Pure Yoga

Pure Yoga

*The Spiritual Heart of Ancient Wisdom:
A Guide to Life for Peace, Health and
Wealth*

Pooran

ori·pace

Yoga is the original state of peace and stillness where Consciousness flows freely. In this state of peace and serenity, the mind reflects its true potential

Patanjali, the Yoga Sutras

"This book is beyond radical. Radical means pertaining to the roots or foundation. This book claims there is no such thing as roots or foundation. There is only the utter clarity of reality as it is. And that is exactly what I have found to be the case.

This book may shake up what you think you understand. And that is a good thing."

Joey Lott author of Peace Feels Like This and You're Trying to Hard

Openings

PART 1

IN THE BEGINNING

The world post-Covid has changed radically. We have realised that the old ways are not working anymore and must adapt to a new society. As work patterns and lifestyles change radically, new opportunities arise. Our challenge is to recognise these new opportunities and harness them to our individual and collective potential.

This book is a roadmap to our bright future, taking guidance from the past, using the wisdom of ancient sages and adapting to the modern age. It reconnects to Yoga's spiritual core. The practice and exercises are transformative, opening up a world of infinite possibilities and potential.

Yoga has always had mystical and spiritual elements that the physical practice often overlooks, favouring a more postural emphasis. A deep meditative spirituality characterised the earliest Yoga practice back in the heartlands of India thousands of years ago.

The spiritual practice of Yoga is the ultimate self-help tool to develop a clear awareness of oneself and greater clarity of thought. With enhanced understanding, the yoga practitioner is no longer the victim of external problems but controls their destiny.

Spiritual Yoga liberates us from restrictive social conditioning to live a life of fulfilment and joy. The body is purified of the negative mental energy that obstructs the kundalini flow through *the chakras*, developing a healthy mind in a healthy body.

The benefits of Pure Yoga soon become apparent. You develop confidence. Your face radiates joy and charisma, and your body becomes light. Your enhanced awareness increases your potential to succeed in your chosen field of expertise and recognise new opportunities.

By deepening their experience of the spiritual aspects of the practice, Yoga teachers and students alike can enrich their knowledge of the different approaches to their practice, including the Yogas of Lifestyle, Knowledge and Devotion.

Pure Yoga is a union between the transient material world and higher Consciousness, a direct experience of a timeless reality. This experience is transcendental. In transcendence comes revival and rebirth, joy, and love.

Pure Yoga is a path towards enlightenment that transcends traditional world knowledge while anchored in the physical world. Therefore, this aspect of Yoga practice is ultra-dimensional and mystic.

This book will guide you to achieving higher Consciousness through daily exercises, starting at five minutes, gradually increasing to an hour. These are exercises in awareness of life's mysteries and wonder. The goal is to unleash your potential as a human being through a process of reappraisal and transcendence.

In Sanskrit, the mother tongue of Yoga it is said: *Raha raha*. Whatever remains, remains. When the Yogi has transcended the limitations of the world, there remains your true self, magnificent and glorious.

OPENING

The Oracle at Delphi said, know yourself. According to the Indian guru Ramana Maharshi of the last century, the only valid question in life is to ask who am I? Who exactly is the person that looks within for an answer to life's mysteries?

Most people don't know themselves. We may have an idea of who we think we are, a self-image and identity. Is that really who we are? Or is it an illusion?

Our self-identity is a hotel. Every room is booked by our multitudes of conditionings. When Consciousness comes calling, there is no room at the inn.

A great Indian Sage, Shankara, said that the philosophy of Yoga teaches that we all have a fully functioning tool to discover to know our true nature. That tool is the mind. We must break down everything that we take for granted, challenging traditional knowledge and defying orthodoxy. We must challenge the supremacy of the mind itself but not dismiss the intellect. We must use our innate reason and intellect to transcend the ordinary mind to find the potential to succeed within us.

The fully expanded intellect has a single purpose: to assist the mind in tuning into a higher consciousness and opening the mind up to what it cannot grasp by any other means. The yogi – a Yoga student- can reach a level of awareness that culminates in higher Consciousness. The mind is then expanded into an ocean of opportunity.

Higher Consciousness is the fundamental principle of Yoga. The practice of spiritual yoga expands limited mind consciousness into an all-encompassing universal consciousness. Life itself becomes Consciousness, God-consciousness, non-dual, all-permeating, in a world of infinite possibilities and potential, the unchanging principle in a complex, changing world.

Most of this will go against the grain and, for many, will challenge your certainties and truisms. We have the highest intelligence because the frontal cerebral cortex gives us a strategic advantage over the rest of the animal, insect, and plant worlds. Consequently, we have appropriated Consciousness as a uniquely human attribute, forgetting that we as a thinking species have existed for only a nano second in the life of the universe.

Consciousness is universal, a field of potentiality, but duality and division inhibit the kundalini flow of potential

Yogis set themselves to merge finite and fallible human experience into infinite reality by developing transcendental Consciousness. Only with an expanded awareness can an individual be truly successful. As a result, the world becomes a network of inter-related experiences, a vista of far greater personal, spiritual, and economic opportunities.

Over many thousands of years, this challenge was met through the growth of ideologies embracing various intellectual positions. There is one common theme throughout this process: we can only experience our life to its highest potential by abandoning any identification with the senses' reality. We can access an expanded reality by identifying our sense of being in this world with higher Consciousness. This reality is ultimately not an experience of anything. It is experience. Life becomes an experience of higher Consciousness, every moment blessed and joyful.

However, to immerse yourself in an experience in hybrid realities is a formidable task. Everything in life pushes us towards the realm of the senses and the mind. As soon as we experience something, we start to think about it, rating it, judging, liking, disliking – or sharing on social media. This is the human condition.

How can we experience anything outside the human condition? Is it even possible? Our intellect mind cannot see the whole picture. Or we see only what is known in Yoga as the relative field, a partial representation of higher Consciousness.

The puzzle of what is real and what is not real begs the following question: if our human reality is an illusion, what then is real, if anything? Because something is clearly happening.

Yoga teaches us that there is just one reality and one experience. This absolute reality is not defined by us. To grasp the concept of a formless reality with the mind requires a higher awareness and suspending disbelief. The intellect is the only tool that can train us to acquire this knowledge and transform the mind into something greater than itself.

We need, therefore, to work on the intellect. This is the starting point, the ground zero for the development of an expanded mind.

Higher Consciousness is our natural state. In the womb, before the world claimed us, we were in tune with Consciousness. As soon as we are born, we experience the relative field as change and division, which blinds us to our birthright. We become entangled in the web of life. Training is required to dissolve the ties that bind and to let the mind be reabsorbed into higher Consciousness. This is the enlightenment experience.

Yoga and its mystic tradition go back thousands of years. The natural world influenced the analogies that the yogi sages used: light dispels darkness, brightness brings enlightenment, an illusion is a poison. The illusion of the rope seen as a snake in the dark is a classic analogy.

Nowadays, light pollution obscures the stars in the night sky. None of that existed back then on the Indian subcontinent when Yoga evolved. So the analogy of the lamp of wisdom is compelling and immediate.

Enlightenment is a transformation of darkness to light, from confusion to clarity of mind. An enlightened person clearly sees the path to take in life, all doubt and confusion removed.

With practice, a spiritual Yogi clearly sees the moment that one reality is transformed into another. The source of our different experiences becomes evident, as do the hidden potentialities.

An opening is a term used in Yoga to describe a shift in Consciousness. It is walking through a door into a new psychological panorama, making first contact with higher Consciousness, like a prisoner released from the cage of a former existence, once free, forever free.

We bow to the gurus of India, the mother ship of enlightenment and self-realisation. Our debt and gratitude are immense.

Om is a sacred sound and an icon in Dharmic religions and philosophies. It is also a mantra in Yoga, Buddhism and Jainism.

In classic Indian tradition, Om is a symbol referring to both Atman (the soul, self within) and Brahman (the ultimate reality, the entirety of the universe, the one truth, and the supreme spirit).

The syllable is an important symbol in Indian spiritual practice, found at the beginning and the end of chapters in the Vedas, the Upanishads, and the Yoga Sutras. Om is a mantra chanted during the recitation of spiritual texts and meditative activities.

Exercise 1

Awareness of Sound

This exercise should be done with the eyes closed, though eyes open also works.

Five minutes

Be aware of sound. Simply be mindful that sound exists, independent of what we are hearing. Whatever is being listened to is sound. Take time off from associating sound with things and objects and creating more associations with other things and objects. Instead, be aware of Pure Sound.

Use a timer. Best done first thing in the morning and early evening, though the exercise can be done at any time and as many times.

This is an exercise in observation and awareness, the first step to realising higher Consciousness.

Benefits: This exercise gradually sharpens the intellect as the mind becomes more flexible in its response to external stimuli.

THE ANCIENT SCIENCE OF YOGA

WHAT IS THE POINT OF YOGA? In Sanskrit, the ancient language of India, the word '*artha*' means purpose, meaning or sense. This Sanskrit word, from the prototype Indo-European language, some seven thousand years old, is the distant descendant of the English word 'art'. Yoga is art. Yoga is purpose. Yoga is meaning. Yoga is the art of living and engaging with the world.

The essence of the human condition is involvement with the external world of material phenomena. We give value and meaning to everything that we experience through the senses. Consequently, everything seems so real.

Silence is never silent for long, if at all. Thoughts are like frogs croaking in the mind. This is loop thought processing.

The brain is overloaded processing incoming data. It becomes impossible to see the wood for the trees.

Many thousands of years ago, mystics experienced a deathless state, neither 'here' nor 'there'. In this state, questions and answers exist in perfect harmony. Logically a question comes before the response. If you change the question, the answer will change accordingly. A question without an explanation is left hanging. A solution without question does not relate to anything or anyone. But what if there exists an undivided state in which both question and answer are the same?

When does cause become the effect, or is it a continuum of co-existing possibilities, any one of which can be chosen? Pure Yoga increases our ability to determine both the path we take and the end goal.

Those ancient mystics recognised that a state that bypasses question and answer and cause and effect cannot be expressed intellectually in words. It must be experienced,

They started analysing the world around them, the one they could breathe and feel - elemental and three dimensional, all causally related.

These ancient truth seekers didn't have much to go by. No computers to process data or microscopes to go deep into the elements of nature. Their technology was not up to much: wheels, pulleys, levers and gears. They didn't even have proper windows. But they had plenty of time, and they could chant their sacred mantras under a starlit heavenly sky, in a state of wonder and awe. So they retreated to the mountains or entered deep into the forest to pursue their mystic quest.

These yogis realised that the mind coalesces reality into little packets of comfortable familiarity. That the intellect polarises everything into opposites: rain and sunshine, pain and pleasure, life and death, love and hatred, peace and violence, man and woman, child and adult, week and weekend, day and night, sunrise and sunset, now and then, me and you, us and them. It is no wonder that people resort to rigid ideas of who they are, even if this means shutting down potential and opportunity.

But they also realised we have the innate ability to understand what lies beyond the division and harness unlimited potential. This ability is our birthright, one that is overlooked in the struggle of life.

These truth-seekers deconstructed their sense of self-identity fabricated from personal experiences that the brain had bundled up from selective memories. They traced the development of self-identity conditioned by external circumstances and a set of likes and dislikes, influenced by arbitrary cultural and personal preferences that merge and solidify into an individual personality.

Most people have very little control over this process. Our self-identity is mainly down to chance and social conditioning. The ancient yogis saw this as the limiting principle in life that needs to be overcome to expand the mind for greatness.

Next, these ancient yogis asked themselves: what remains, and what happens to self-identity when the body dies? Is it just a case of now you see it, now you don't?

The first yogis lived in an age when spirit gods were considered intermediaries between the word of mortals and the divine realm. These gods merged into a monotheistic entity, an all-knowing and omnipotent God. However, God acted in ways that could not be easily explained. Why all the suffering?

No logical solution to suffering proved entirely satisfactory.

The ancient yogis turned to meditation, looking within rather than to the heavens. Their self-inquiry led to the Darshana Santana, the Eternal Philosophy, which recognises the innate human faculty of Consciousness.

Increasingly, modern societies accept that spiritual Consciousness is a valid human experience, and that Yoga is a channel for higher Consciousness. Thousands of years after the first yogis conducted their thought experiments, their research findings have reached global acceptance and validation.

Meditation has become increasingly popular in the last century Yoga is not the only spiritual tradition that sets out to achieve a transcended state of mind. Still, it is one of the most documented. Part of the mass appeal of Yoga is that it is not a belief system that might jar with religious systems. The one moral absolute is *ahimsa*, the principle of non-violence.

To unlock the mind's potential, Yogis distinguished between causal and transcendent reality. *Causal reality* means the conditioned world where everything and everyone impacts everything and everyone else. Yogis sought to transcend this chain of events by merging human Consciousness into a causeless flux of existence or non-causal reality. It is in this transcendence that the individual's potential lies.

Transcended Consciousness cannot be defined purely intellectually. Pure Yoga is mystic in nature and is not an intellectual experience. The super-mind embraces contradiction and does not rely on rational thought or the intellect to validate a self-evident truth. Transcended Consciousness is intuitive knowledge of multiple realities.

According to the ancient yogis, all truths are true and not true at the same time. This contradictory co-existence is now defined as *polar logic* – embracing both opposites of a logical argument simultaneously. Nothing is entirely true or false, merely relative to a single higher truth. To embrace opposing logic, one must have a flexible mind.

Thousands of years ago, sadhus, truth-seekers, realised that the rational mind was anchored to the three-dimensional world of a space-time continuum. Today, humans are slaves to reason. Thus, logic and the faculty of reason justify human behaviour, even when it appears illogical. But is logic all that it is cracked up to be?

What's the matter with this cruel world today?

Ideologies infect nations and cultures with an irrational impulse for violence. Logic caused over two hundred million deaths in wars in the last century alone. It was organised slaughter. The total mortality of World War I, World War II, and the Russian Civil War were 80 million, 16% of all Europeans dead due to warfare. War and genocide are regularly carried out by governments acting irrationally in the name of logic, carried out by reasonable people. Without logistics, war cannot be waged.

The disease of war feeds off the logical mind. 13 million face starvation in Yemen because of a genocidal war between two opposing political ideologies, and it all seems so rationally reasonable to sell both sides weapons. The logic of war justified the atomic bombing of Hiroshima and Nagasaki. Terrorists used a perverse logic to fly planes into the Twin Towers.

You can't solve a problem with the same level of Consciousness that identified the problem.

Those early Indian yogis realised that logic is never absolute but subservient to higher universal Consciousness. From the Yoga perspective, *everything* in the human experience is relative and conditioned, including logic and reason. Nothing in the physical realm is by itself a stand-alone truth. And this is because things only *appear* to be real. Logic only *seems* to be logical.

Our sense of reality is an illusion. Reality is neither true nor false. All truth is relative.

❁

There are four levels of logic: low, medium, high and transcendental.

Low-level logic is the everyday logic of how things operate in *the realm of the mechanical.* Do this, and that happens.

Medium logic governs the decisions we make as we go about our daily business. It is a matter of individual choice. *The realm of the personal.*

High-level logic is ideological and conceptual. Pro Brexit or Remain. Democrat or Republican. Apple or Android. Pro- and anti-vaxers have their own reasons to justify their belief. The seeds of division are sown here. Conflict often ensues in *the realm of belief systems.*

Transcendental logic is observational, neither involved or uninvolved with cause or effect, right or wrong. We are merely aware in *the realm of Higher Consciousness.*

Exercise 2

Five minutes Awareness of Logic

This exercise can be done with the eyes open or closed. It makes no difference. It is an exercise in awareness.

Be aware of the force of logic in your life. Do not evaluate the rights and wrongs or the consequences. Simply be mindful that logic exists.

Use a timer. Best done first thing in the morning and early evening, though the exercise can be done at any time and as many times.

This is an exercise in observation and awareness, the second step to realising higher Consciousness.

Benefits:

Increased awareness of the realm of the mechanical, the base level of logic. Clarity of thought and insight into thought processes.

THE ORIGINS OF YOGA

Yoga today is mainstream, but yogic practices originated in mystic rituals dedicated to the goddess Kali many thousands of years ago. It was nothing like the yoga we know today. Yoga was initially a visceral and intense practice.

Kali was a god worshipped as the mother of life and death by a sect called the *Aghoris* living at the confines of civilisation near cemeteries. Aghoris based their beliefs on two principles: that Kali is all-knowing, ever-present and all-powerful, the primal cause of absolutely everything in the universe, in all dimensions, manifest and unmanifest. Consequently, everything that exists in the world must be perfect. To deny the inherent perfection of anything was to deny the sanctity of all life in its full manifestation. Even death is perfect. Not fearing death was the mark of a devotee to the Goddess Kali.

A fierce warrior cult devoted to Kali developed. The concept of the body as a temple of worship became integral to the practices of the Kali cult.

Yoga poses were initially militaristic. A primitive form of *Hatha* Yoga gradually evolved. This less aggressive form of Yoga was adapted to accommodate local cultures and deities. As society developed structures, it marginalised the death cult associations. A priestly caste took control, asserting the supremacy of sacred texts. Yoga became less extreme, more socially acceptable and accessible to the ordinary householder. The fierce Yogis became bodyguards to the literate elite and acted as protective warriors of this new society.

The yogis carefully codified the secrets of the practice. The performance aspects of this tradition were ritualised, becoming increasingly sophisticated and civilised. First orally and later in scriptures, the arcane mysteries of uniting life and death and merging physical matter with spirit morphed into teachings of a higher existence. The literate intelligentsia taught the new philosophies in stone carved temples. Still, wild monks, their skin daubed in grey funeral ash and faces painted orange, preserved Yoga's origins in the cult of Kali.

The first references to Yoga are in the Vedas, a set of mystical writings in verse form composed four thousand years ago.

In the Vedas, the cosmos had a natural order. The early gods equated with the forces of nature. Humanity was utterly at the mercy of the gods who were not bound by morality. These gods were powerful entities, and so it was sensible to curry favour with them. Piety was a practical solution to the seemingly chaotic nature of the world. It was prudent to offer holy sacrifices if you wanted the gods to look after your family.

Mantras developed from superstitious spells.

The spiritual core of Yoga developed in the broader Indian tradition, which spanned two distinct civilisations, the Aryan North and the Shivait South. Some of the earliest writings in the history of humanity originate in the culture of the Indus valley of the northwest region of India in the Bronze Age period 3300-1300 BCE. This era was the big bang of human Consciousness, which heralded a flowering of higher thought processes all over the planet.

Little is known about how people lived in the Indus Valley. However, archaeological findings have shown that their civilisation was sophisticated and refined.

Their sages envisioned an infinite universe extending beyond the observable night sky. Western science only caught up with this relatively recently. Until the 1920's astronomers maintained that our universe did not extend beyond our Galaxy, the Milky Way.

This ancient culture produced the Vedas and the Upanishads, sacred scriptures transmitted orally through generations and later in writing mainly in Sanskrit. The oral tradition includes songs of poetry and philosophy called *gitas*. The most famous is the Bhagavad Gita that tells of a conversation between Krishna and Arjuna on the eve of a tremendous inter-familial battle. Prince Arjuna is having a psychological crisis at the prospect of having to kill old friends and relatives the next day on the battlefield - and possibly lose his life in the process.

This Gita is part of an epic, the Mahabharata. Krishna, the charioteer of Prince Arjuna, is no ordinary charioteer but an avatar of the world's creator. This is a work of spiritual philosophy that underpinned a sophisticated and cultured society. Its rhyming meter contains 32 syllables in each verse, which gives the Gita a hypnotic quality when sung.

Krishna represents Higher Conscious, while Prince Arjuna represents humanity, confused, bewildered, and lost, trapped in human Consciousness. Krishna explains to Arjuna how he should act in the world and gives a comprehensive exposition of the principal schools of Indian philosophy.

He tells Arjuna that he needs to understand that he is not killing anyone on the battlefield because there is nobody to be killed. Life and death are all part of the big illusion. Suppose Arjuna thinks that he is the one killing. In that case, he will be plagued by fear and doubt, which guarantees misery, regardless of the outcome. Although there will be violence on the battlefield, the true essence of his nature is not involved. Arjuna needs to realise he is the Eternal Self uninvolved with the human drama unfolding. Everyone – and everything -is a manifestation of the Eternal and Immortal Self.

One might expect that the principle of non-violence (*ahimsa*) would dictate that Arjuna should not fight and turn the other cheek to these injustices rather than fight. However, that is not the way forward because his opponents mean him and his people harm. Arjuna needs to engage.

Krishna tells Arjuna to give up self-identification with the fruits of his actions. The people he sees in the opposing army, his teachers, friends, and relatives, are all manifestations of a higher consciousness unidentified with what will happen on the battlefield.

The person who thinks that this Higher Consciousness causes the killing or can be destroyed has not grasped the truth because the True Self neither kills nor is killed.

Higher Consciousness is not subject to birth or death. Even when it has become manifest in some form or other, seemingly having been born, the truth is that Consciousness remains eternal. When a body appears to be killed, it is only the earthly form that changes.

So, Arjuna, as you now know, the Self or God is eternal and not subject to changes of the physical form. Therefore, there is no need to worry that you will be killed or grieve for the dead.

The Self, manifest in a physical form, just casts off that form, like changing clothes. Nothing changes. There is only the appearance of change.

Nothing affects the Self. It is immortal and indestructible.

Always keep God in mind as eternal, omniscient, unmoving, ever-present. The Self is unmanifest, beyond our comprehension, beyond change. So do not worry or fear, Arjuna.

Exercise 3

Ten minutes Awareness of Higher Consciousness

This exercise can be equally done with eyes closed or open. With eyes closed is closer to the meditative experience and is more focused on mental awareness. If doing with eyes open, it is best to fix on a single point. The awareness is more visual.

The point of this exercise is to start to 'know' higher Consciousness. Gradually an awareness rises that there is a greater power observing what's going on. A higher being is present in your life. You are that.

There is no need to define this experience. Just be aware that this is your higher self.

Ideally, twice a day. Aim for fifteen minutes, longer if possible.

Benefits: Increased awareness of the realm of the personal – how we relate to the world in our uniquely individual way. No two people are alike, but we all share the same consciousness which is the well spring of our potential and success.

HIGHER GROUND

The battle scene with Krishna and Arjuna is in the Bhagavad Gita part of a literary epic. The Mahabharata belongs to the heroic age like the Odyssey, the Iliad and the Epic of Gilgamesh, which features tribal feuds, family dramas and violent confrontations between heroes and villains and superheroes.

The dramatic confrontation with imminent death allows Arjuna to epiphany the truth of his existence and his whole assumed reason for existence. Krishna dismantles Arjuna's self-identity, freeing him up to re-identify with higher Consciousness.

Krishna tells Aruna to be more than a man. Be a God.

The battle represents an extreme situation. In such moments of high drama, people are open to revelations and insight. Krishna's dilemma could be any problematic situation that we face in life.

The epic Mahabharata introduces *Pashupati*, an ascetic belief system centring on the God Shiva as a Yogi. As in Buddhism, the end of unhappiness and existential angst - *dukkhanta* - is the goal of the yogi's existence. Krishna is an avatar of Shiva.

Krishna was initially a boy god worshipped by native tribes before the Aryan invasion. His libertine attitude reflected his status as a fertility god. He was a warrior king before acquiring divine status in the Bhagavad Gita.

The Bhagavad Gita is a synthesis of the different philosophical and theological strands of its era. It does not adhere to a single doctrinal or philosophical ideology. At times, the gist of the Gita is monistic, one god; other times, it's pantheistic, that is, many gods. It both encourages respect for the tradition of the Vedas, the earliest writings in the mystic tradition, but elsewhere suggests they are useless. Devotion to a monotheist god is recommended, while an undercurrent of atheism runs through the verses. The Bhagavad Gita embraces contradiction, always challenging comfortable orthodoxy.

Indian spirituality, for all the elephant and monkey gods and temple doors with all sorts of wild sex depicted on stone carvings, is intellectually rigorous. Core to the Bhagavad Gita is the concept of a knower (*ksetrajna*) that knows the mental and material worlds. This knower is the infinite self, a witness or spectator to the world, a non-doer. The subjective experience is the unchanging essence of all change.

The Bhagavad Gita is essentially a hybrid of religion, philosophy and cosmic exploration. Krishna is a god-like figure and a guru. Prince Arjuna comes to understand that the absolute cannot be comprehended by thought because of the limited capacity of his mind. The world can only be understood in terms of a divine mystery *or Maya*. He can only be free of an imperfect reality through a mystic experience. Krishna is an avatar of Shiva sent to explain that mystery.

The Bhagavad Gita introduces the concept of the avatar as a divine manifestation sent as a world redeemer. This idea of an avatar descending to save humanity was recycled in Christianity. Krishna and Christ both manifest from God into a human incarnation. In Christianity, the concept of *Maya*, the grand illusion, is replaced by the idea of sin. The avatar reveals to humanity their full potential by transcending their flaws and becoming Krishna or Christ.

The Bhagavad Gita was written about 400 hundred years before Jesus lived. Jesus might even have lived in India, and his teachings were influenced by the Gita.

Krishna introduces Arjuna to the concepts of *Yogah karmasu kaushalam,* efficiency in action and *samatva-buddhi,* mental balance.

Be steady in Yoga, Arjuna, do whatever has to be done; give up attachment, be indifferent to failure and success. Mental balance is Yoga.

A balanced mind is not motivated by desire; defend your mind with mental balance and poise, Arjuna. People who are obsessed with the results of their actions are prone to error.

With mental poise, you will be free from worrying about what is right and what is wrong. Devote yourself to this Yoga; it is the secret of success in everything you do.

Krishna refers to Yoga as a higher mind, an intelligence that is indifferent to results but still engaged in action.

The Bhagavad Gita also contains several notions of Indian thought fundamental to Yoga: the concept of *Maya* as an illusion, the psychology of Yoga, the philosophical system of philosophy called *Samkhya*, the lifestyle of *karma* and the knowledge of *gyan*[1].

There are six main branches of Indian philosophy: the six *orthodox* systems and three *non conformists* (or heterodox) systems. The two conventional systems that have continued to flourish are the Yoga and Advaita schools, which share many underlying assumptions on the nature of existence and diverge in other aspects. For example, Yoga is the union of human conscious multiplicities with a single all-pervading infinite reality. In contrast, Advaita is a non-dualist philosophy that holds that there is just one Consciousness.

Buddhism, the third of the major themes of Indian thought, evolved as a non-conformist philosophy. It was a reaction to many of the dogmas prevalent in the Indian sub-continent circa 500 pre-CE.

One of the Buddha's first teachers was a teacher of the extreme ascetic yoga tradition. The Buddha almost starved to death going down the route of asceticism before adopting the 'middle path' between extremes.

---

[1] *Also spelt Jnana.*

In time, Buddhism split into many different schools. *Theravada* adhered to the original teachings of the Buddha as recorded orally. It was passed down the centuries by generations of *bikkhus* (monks). *Mahayana* expanded on the original Buddhist canon, introducing the concept of a non-dual zero, the sunyata. Amongst the many competing Buddhist academies, there was even a Yoga school of Buddhism, the Yogacara. Finally, the philosophical basis for Mahayana was established by Nagarjuna. This is Buddhism that we associate with Tibet and Japan.

The school of *Advaita* started to gain ground from the fifth century CE. Advaita essentially means *not two* or non-dual. *'A'* means 'not', and *'Dva'* is two. Advaita is a philosophy of non-duality.

Vedanta quite simply means the end of the Vedas, the mystical poems from pre-history. It proclaims that Vedanta is the culmination of the earliest Vedic teachings.

The hybrid Advaita Vedanta has become the default spiritual system of most modern Indian gurus. Moreover, Advaita Vedanta is the basis of Transcendental Meditation.

The Vedanta system of philosophy now has various branches. The differences are in how much they adhere to or diverge from the concept of non-dualism. There is 'qualified' dualism and 'strict dualism' and, if that was not enough dualisms, there is a *'neither dualist nor non-dualist,* school. They disagree on some facets of Vedanta but mostly all preach that *moksha,* unity with the One, is the goal of life. Every situation, every question, and every predicament can be synthesised into an experience of Higher Consciousness.

Krishna explains to Arjuna in the Bhagavad Gita that his sense of existing as a unique individual is called *Asmita* - an approximation is 'I am-ness'. All sentient creatures have a sense of being, even flowers and plants. Individual *Asmita* is based on sense impressions, memory, and genetics.

Yogis have long taught that a person can experience lasting happiness by becoming aware of the infinite Consciousness in everything. Thus, through the practice of meditation, a personal reality is experienced as an unchanging, indivisible, and infinite consciousness.

Yoga and Advaita Vedanta emerged from a shared philosophical system - Samkhya. From the 19th century, the Yoga and Advaita schools started to merge, incorporating additional influences drawn from the Shiva and Vishnu religions. As a result, modern Yoga gurus are predominantly Advaita teachers, mixed with other strands of Hindu spiritual tradition, the Upanishads and the Vedas.

Exercise 4

Asmita – self-identity

This exercise is with eyes closed and open. The practice is slightly different.

With eyes closed, this is more meditative. Be aware of your sense of being someone- your I-am-ness. Before your self-identity. Your sense of existence is a person who knows the world. Find that I-am-ness and stay with it

Do not get distracted by your thoughts or your name. Just enjoy the experience of being alive without all the stuff that gets attached to you.

The experience of asmita is not to be described or explained. It is both individual and universal. You have no name.

Be aware of the entity that is experiencing the world passing by. This is your I-am-ness. Stay with that this. Let the world be, without you intervening with thought or judgement. Just experience and be aware of your conditionings in *the realm of Belief*

Ten minutes each time.

Benefits:

The ability to disassociate sense of yourself from your conditioned self-identity and transform into someone greater. With practice you become that you are in a state of pure existence rather than just existing as someone who is often motivated by unconscious desires and fears and conditions.

The Shiva Samhita and Hatha Yoga

An early exposition of modern postural Yoga is in the Shiva Samhita from the 15th century, one of the best treatises on yogic science, despite some implausible claims about the benefits of Yoga. In the Shiva Samhita, a yogi can hold the breath for hours on end, rest the body's weight on one thumb, be free from disease, decay, asthma, fly, talk to animals, and finally defeat death.

The Shiva Samhita excels in its descriptions of the breathing practice of *pranayama*, the *asanas* and *mudras*, and meditation. Reading these words is to be transported back in time to an age of yogis doing their exercises with the single goal – to achieve synthesis with the Cosmos without superimposing the senses or mind interference. The mission statement is evident in the opening lines.

'There is one true knowledge without beginning or end. No other real entity exists. The diversity in this world appears through the imposition of the senses on knowledge and for no other reason.'

One particularly exotic practice is semen retention and drawing up female ejaculate as if this were divine milk through the urethra. A detailed description on how to do this is included in the Shiva Samhita. Don't try that in your local yoga class.

The guru in the Shiva Samhita is intensely revered. True and faithful practice of the Shiva Samhita absolves the yogi of all sins, including sleeping with the guru's wife. As a result of intense practise, the yogi not only gains superhuman powers but becomes, somewhat implausibly, a sex magnet.

'At the sight of the practitioner who repeats this mantra one hundred thousand times, women tremble and become sick with lust. They fall shameless before the yogi.'

It is not clear what effect female yogis (*yoginis*) have upon men.

The Shiva Samhita takes credulity to the limit in its overblown claims of the benefits of Yoga, but to dismiss these extraordinary claims would be to miss the truism that flows throughout the verses, contained succinctly in the first verse: *there is just one truth, one Consciousness, and the rest is all imagination.*

Seeing duality.

Duality is the default operational protocol in the human experience.

From childhood, a person comes to necessarily learn that the world is real. Knowledge, experience, and a sense of the world are inextricably linked. When you start to question the very nature of knowledge itself, a question inevitably arises. What exactly is true?

Yoga offers a boldly original explanation of the human condition

Our sense of reality is dependent on time to be coherent. Time is a requisite. But is there a reality that exists timelessly before birth, during life and after death? And how then to describe this reality without resorting to the usual reference points in time and space?

Advaita philosophy identifies three elementary states of experience the *waking state*, *the dream state* and the *dreamless state*. At any one time, a person lives in one of these three states.

Contemporary science uses a different language altogether, explaining brain states as silent neocortical neurons measured in hertz or slow-wave sleep. Different wave patterns determine our conscious awareness.

Yoga proposes that what passes for human Consciousness in the three states is simply a continuum of degrees of awareness. Higher Consciousness operates on an entirely different level, in both the sentient and the insentient objects.

The human brain is just not programmed to accept any other reality than what is presented to it. Reality is *species-specific*. We experience the world with the senses.

Illusion permeates the waking state. The six senses do not tell the whole truth. Instead, they spin a version of a factual reality that is wholly convincing but not entirely real.

The mind is the sixth sense. It creates a perception of a single reality from various influences and associations: from things seen, touched, heard, tasted and smelt, to memories from previous experience.

Exercise 5

The sixth sense and duality

Be aware of the mind in operation. Do not conclude or judge. Awareness is open-ended, a string of moments in a continuum.

With eyes closed, be aware of the associations that give meaning and value. How the mind gives rise to a sense of self from I-am-ness. The likes and dislikes, the preferences, and aversions. Do not go too deep into the mind – just be aware that you have a sense of mind, and that mind is not you.

With eyes open, see how a sixth sense is constantly processing the world. Observe the mind as a process, reacting, associating, conceptualising and objectifying,

This is the continuum of the realms of the *mechanical, personal and belief* systems transcending ordinary Consciousness.

Mediate for thirty minutes

Benefits

If you mediate to hide from the world, you will be a person who hides from the world.

If you mediate to engage the world, you will become vibrant and charismatic.

By being aware of your mind as your sixth sense, you open a door. You engage with the world on a deeper and more meaningful way

TRANSCENDENCE

The concept that the world is a manifestation of higher Consciousness is fundamental to the spiritual practice of Yoga.

There is no single reality, just an illusory experience of multiple tangible realities. A succession of events is linked together. A healthy brain can create a collage of these shapes, forms and happenings and transform this into a cohesive personal reality. No two truths are identical.

This constructed reality is *mithya*, a myth. All lives are lived as epics.

However, an elevated state of Consciousness transcends the apparent reality of everyday experience when the mind enters a superstate of Pure Awareness.

In this state of Consciousness, known in Sanskrit as *turiya*, the mind is free from self-imposed limitations. The ability to enter the state of turiya is innate, a dormant feature hidden deep in human Consciousness. The practise of spiritual yoga awakens this sleeping dragon.

The experience of *turiya*, the transcended mind, is essentially mystical, an epiphany state, a breaking through to the other side

In *turiya*, the illusion of being separate from the universe is dissolved, like ice cubes in water. Instead, knowledge, awareness, and Consciousness merge into one superstate of existence, transcending a world divided by belief and prejudice.

The transcended mind soars into the sky. Potential and opportunities abound. The intellect has fulfilled its purpose: to allow the mind to be suffused in potential and greatness and individual talent to flourish.

THE YOGA OF MEDITATION

You have to do your own work;
Enlightened Ones will only show the way.
Those who practice meditation
Will free themselves from their chain.
Dhammapada 20.276

Meditation is a totally unique practice in that nothing is being done. However, the brain, consisting of a synaptic system and a neuronal network, continually fires up mental activity.

Some people, initially, feel they must come away from meditation with something positive - a lesson, a reward, a victory. The practice of meditation is not goal orientated. There is no agenda, no pre-determined goals according to a plan.

There is no right or wrong way.

Meditation is not a formula that can be trademarked. No one size fits all, not every day and not for each occasion.

Meditation is not an exercise in mind control. Nor is it about thinking with the eyes closed or ridding the mind of thoughts. Meditation essentially is about finding a sense of balance and equilibrium without trying to control the flow of sensations that arise. One way of doing this is to observe the mind in action and see what it throws up. This approach is the basis of mindfulness meditation.

Meditation is not for everybody. Neuroses and psychological complexes may surface from the unconscious to the conscious mind. For example, people with obsessive tendencies can find themselves giving validation to phobias and fears, thereby reinforcing them. Rather than feeling relieved, people can become confused, seeing and hearing things that are not there. The impact on an unstable mind can be distressing. Children are particularly vulnerable.

With training, however, such phobias can be seen for what they are: mental constructs. Yogis can meditate for many hours on end. In Tibet, monks meditate in the snow. In addition, there is a Tibetan tradition of monks and nuns immured into a cave for many years, meditating blissfully.

In 1976 Tenzin Palmo commenced living in a cave in the Himalayas measuring 10 feet wide and six feet deep and remained there for 12 years, for three of which she was in full retreat. The cave was high in the remote Lahaul area of the Indian Himalayas, on the border of Himachal Pradesh and Tibet. She grew her own food and practised deep meditation based on ancient Buddhist beliefs. Following strict protocol, she never lay down, sleeping in a traditional wooden meditation box in a meditative posture for just three hours a night. She spent the last three years in complete isolation and survived temperatures of below −30° Fahrenheit (−35°C) and snow for six to eight months of the year.

It is not advisable to start extended meditation practice without a framework. The Yoga Sutras of Patanjali opens with a remarkably concise line in Sanskrit: *Yogash chitt vritti nirodah. The state of Yoga occurs when the waves of the mind are still.* It lays down a marker for what follows.

Yogash is the state of Yoga.
Chitt is Consciousness.
Vritti are the modifications or mind waves.
Nirodah is the cessation or stilling.

The highest state of Yoga is reached when the mind waves no longer impact Consciousness. Yoga becomes the transcended state of peace and stillness where intelligence flows freely.

Consciousness is already still. The wave of existence is always still. This stillness is our natural state of being. The mind desires nothing and goes nowhere: *you are immersed in your true self.*

When not in this original state of stillness of a cosmic mind, our minds are caught up in the stream of relative Consciousness.

Fundamental to the concept of a cosmic mind is *saaroopyam*, meaning identification or entanglement. The waves of cosmic Consciousness become entangled with mental energy reacting to the world of objects, things and desires. Internal conflicts then influence the states of the mind as thoughts pile up on each other, associating with previous experiences and conditioning.

Meditation frees the mind of this conditioning. The *ahankaar* is the inner actor who experiences the world. This actor can disassociate with the conditioned mind and reassociate with a higher Consciousness.

In meditation, nothing is being achieved, just a calling to the mind of a greater sense of self. Recalling the higher self is *nididhyasana*, allowing the stream of thoughts to flow in a state of non-attachment. A lifestyle lived with Nididhyasana opens up the world to new possibilities of experience, living in an external state of flux while remaining in harmony with an unchanging consciousness.

Awareness or mindfulness

Mindfulness is the most popular type of meditation promoted. Being aware is not the same as being mindful. The difference is that in awareness meditation, the mind does not engage with the objects of meditation. We become simply aware without drawing any conclusions or conducting any analysis. Things just are. The mind will inevitably rationalise as this is what our brains do. We can be aware of the wind or our fears. We learn to be mindful of our moods and emotions. Eventually, we become aware of the mind in action.

There is no clear demarcation between what awareness means and what is meant by mindfulness. The Buddhists tend to use mindfulness as a translation of *sati,* one of the eight noble truths. The Yoga Sutras speak of *nirbeej samadhi,* formless contemplation.

Exercise 6

Awareness of thought

Close your eyes to filter out visual stimulation. Observe how thoughts associate with memory, sound and other thoughts, creating a sequence of ideas and images. Do you have control over this process? Generally, not. Most people think without really knowing why.

The gist of this exercise is not to control your thoughts or the mind, but simply to be aware of what's going on. In time, a guiding principle becomes apparent – the power of association. And your ability to associate with ever more profound levels of experience opens up hitherto hidden fields of potential and opportunity.

This does not happen overnight – it can take months or even years of practice to expand your mind's associative processes. However, you will soon notice how your thoughts manipulate what you do and how many of these thoughts are planted in your psyche by external forces: family, religion, media, social elements.

Benefits

Awareness of your thoughts is the single most powerful tool in your toolbox when constructing a new reality for yourself. You will develop clarity of thought and a renewed sense of purpose in the long term. In the short term, you will experience a lightness of mind as you decouple your thoughts from the external factors that have limited you in fulfilling your potential.

THE YOGA OF LIFESTYLE-KARMA

Karma are actions, both mental and physical.

Karma is often misunderstood to be the result or consequence of actions. Karma simply means effort or conscious doing or thinking and is one of the building blocks of personality. All karma originates in the mind.

In the Yoga of Lifestyle, karma is the work that helps your mind stay in the yogic field.

Even thinking is a conscious action. Thoughts are mental actions, mental karma, and these can stay in the realm of thought or transform into physical activities.

Every conscious mental action generates a physical reaction, seen or unseen. Karmic Flow is a psychological and physical energy stream with no clear boundary where the psychological and physical fields begin or end. Only the concept of time and space confines the karma flow. For example, a book page reflects a karmic flow of events that started hundreds of billions of years ago when life developed: from waves of Consciousness, molecules and atoms, seed, sapling, tree, woodcutter, pulp, paper, ink, page. All these words are just a moment in this process. Everything is karma.

Yoga karmasu kaushalam is the efficient use of time and effort, the art of doing things in tune with higher Consciousness.

The concept of uninvolved action defines doing things with no attachment to the result of actions. On the path of *karma Yoga,* action becomes the union of two forces: the individual working awareness and its source in cosmic Consciousness, the mind of God.

An uninvolved action produces better results and does not dissipate unnecessary energy. From a business perspective, individual productivity increases when the mind is not made heavy with anticipation and expectation. Actions progress harmoniously when the mind is at one with the actual performance of the task at hand and not restlessly getting ahead of itself. Performance anxiety is detrimental to the result.

Human beings are work animals and possession addicts, continually doing stuff and acquiring things. Just being conscious in the waking state is a form of action. Karma Yoga is simply put a technique of how to work and think skilfully.

Karma and disability

Reincarnation is an idea. Nobody can know for sure, not with our level of science, if there is any reincarnation. So, reincarnation is metaphysical – that is partly scientific, partly conceptual.

Cosmic Consciousness and God are not attached to the body, which is just a psychological organism. The very notion of death is alien to the cosmic mind because it presumes a beginning and an end. The whole point of Yoga is to step off the wheel of birth and death, not to perpetuate existence on the cycle.

Reincarnation with male patriarchy and a class system added is a toxic mix. Such an interpretation of karma is a convoluted cocktail of misogyny, social prejudice, and sheer medieval backwardness. It is an aberration based on an erroneous approach to what constitutes identity. People who hold such views have a superficial understanding of karma. The Self cannot be killed, cut, wind-blown, reduced or deformed, so how can it be reborn?

Exercise 7

Awareness of Karma

Awareness of Consciousness is not measured by facts and figures, nor can it be understood in terms of ideas and concepts.
We can observe the flow of karma in the world, be they human or natural. Cars, voices, wind, leaves rustling, the play of light from the sun. We are aware as an impartial witness who is 'knowing' the world, not judging, but not associating or engaging. Not during this exercise.

Think of it as taking a holiday from yourself. Or watching a film. It is all happening.

Benefits:

Seeing how events are all interlinked and related increase your ability to follow a trail of consequences. This gives insight into the outcomes of your course of action. You experience in the awareness of now a potentiality which becomes manifest in the future,

RAJ YOGA

IN THE TEACHINGS OF YOGA, the approach to knowledge is diametrically opposite to a modern conventional view of what constitutes learning.

Practical knowledge is a product of evolution. Without time and space, there can be no knowledge of the world.

Yogic knowledge – *Gyan* as it is called in Sanskrit - is innate and is the foundation of all subsequent development. Gyan is knowledge of raw existence and not an understanding of facts and data. It is the intelligence that preceded us.

Gyan is not bound to the intellect, but this is not to say that intelligence has no role in Yoga. It is how the mind is used that differs from conventional wisdom. Intellectualising experiences creates a bundle of concepts and big ideas that are helpful but can end up dead.

Gyan is an intuitive experience without a division between subject and object. *Knowledge* always knows us, but the mind is so caught up in a three-dimensional world of multiplicities that we mistake facts for truth.

A Yogic mantra states: Nothing is known that was not already known.

True knowledge is the unconditioned reality in a world of interwoven forms and time, things, places, schedules, facts and figures.

Yoga is a union of earth and sky, *Hatha* Yoga, where all is a flow, *vinyasa*, of energy. There is no separation between what is known and what is still to be known. A formed and unformed reality is yet to become manifest.

There is no distinction between seeking and finding at a transcended level, between understanding and not understanding. On the contrary, freedom not to understand with the intellect is exhilarating and joyful to the expanded mind. Thus, we can rise above the world with all of its contradictions.

The notion of an expanded mind requires *shraddha* - trust or faith. *Shraddha,* as intended here, does not mean trust in anyone or any being, or religion, or belief system or ideology. Instead, it is confidence in a chosen path, a conviction that the fullness of knowledge will evolve in time. The Upanishads, an early mystic text, speak of self-attaining expertise and confidence that the chosen path is right. Just being on the path is to be on the right track. The path is the goal.

Raja

Raja Yoga teaches ways and means to expand the capacity of the intellect. The principle of Raja is that the power and energy of the infinite universe are always available. However, without guidance, people don't know how to access their potential

Conventional education teaches a partial and highly individualised version of reality that is little more than an imposition of social, political, and cultural conditioning. The mental grooves run deep. The older we get, the more conditioned we become, stuck in a deep rut, worn down by unresolved activity. The avenue of potential and opportunity becomes a dead end. Some people become apathetic and give up their quest.

In an unfair and unequal society where racial disparities are oppressive, Raja Yoga is the path to transcend oppression while remaining aware of social injustices. This is because we recognise discrimination but do not become the victim of injustice. Transcending the personal allows the individual to engage and resist from a far greater platform.

Spirit

Knowledge is just *spirit* in action.

Sprit is the conscious life force of both the physical world and unformed reality.

Spirit is the source of all human experience. It permeates every state of invisible and visible existence, including the conscious mind, which grasps the visible and invisible realities. Every meaning, every sound and everything known manifests out of the spirit

Life is the spirit in the body. So wherever there is Consciousness, there is spirit. And because the world is Consciousness, everything is spirit, every thought and action. When we act in this world, we are spirit in action. This spirit guides us to our goals.

The realisation of spirit is the realisation of Raj Yoga. Spirit is *the essence of the human race.* Everyone is born as a physical manifestation of Pure Space. Our *praan* or life force space is contained within the spirit.

The *asanas* or postures of Hatha Yoga allow the spirit to flow unimpeded in the body. Hatha Yoga unleashes the power of Raj Yoga. The mind expands its capacity through the power of nature.

Exercise 7-2

Awareness of Potential

Be aware of how everything is changing every second. This is the principle of change. Even in the elusive timeless Now there is change. And herein lies the power of potential. Be aware of change and trust that in change you will find opportunities.

There is no forcing the issue here. Simply be aware of the flux of existence. It takes practice to not interfere with the process but just let change unfold without our intervention. Eventually, we learn to impartially observe events as they unfold, even if for a limited time of thirty minutes, before diving back into the maelstrom of human activity.

Benefits

As in all the exercises in this book, the benefits are not immediately apparent, but you will get an inkling into further insights as your awareness develops. You may feel destressing as a result of moving yourself from the centre of your mental activity. You may also experience moments of mystic rapture. Gradually you will disassociate yourself from your sense of what you can achieve – and self-imposed limitations - and feel your self-identity expanding. It is in the expanded mind that your potential lies.

RAJ YOGA

Raj Yoga is the pinnacle of our existence, the fulfilment of the true purpose of the mind, to experience *aanand*, the eternal I-consciousness. *Aanand* is mental and spiritual freedom, a state of mind free from doubt, anxiety, and stress, released from wanting more or thinking that something is missing. We are no longer motivated by unrequited desires.

Know yourself, said the Oracle at Delphi. *The Kingdom of God lies within* is from the New Testament. *Be a candle to yourself* comes from the Buddhist scriptures. Knowledge lies within. But in this material, three-dimensional world, where exactly is within? Is this a place, a physical location?

In Indian philosophy, the concept of the Self is paramount. The Self or *Atman* is the physical representation of a higher and perfect whole, the *Brahman*. The goal of human existence is to unite the ordinary mind with transcended Consciousness. However, the ego-intellect mind, the inner actor, creates the illusion of division.

The Self is not to be understood as the Christian concept of the individual Soul – the Self is without any sense of division between the individual and transcended greatness.

The concept of the Self does not feature in Buddhism. The Buddha famously refused to be drawn on any questions about Atman or Brahman, whether there was an eternal self or not, saying enigmatically that the question is not appropriate. However, later Buddhist philosophies known as the Mahayana developed the concept of an eternal Buddha-nature, which is unchanging Self without accepting the existence of an unconditioned absolute being. Thus, for Buddhists, Higher Consciousness is a field of potential in constant flux.

In Advaita, the Self is impersonal, unchanging, and eternal. The Self permeates all the changing and impermanent things of this world. It is in every action, in every thought, in every atom, neutron, and quark and quantum wave. The Self is both here and there, now and then, yesterday, today and tomorrow. The Self never sleeps, permeating both the sentient and insentient world. The Self embraces contradiction because contradiction embraces the whole.

Yoga affirms only Self exists; Consciousness knows the Self; the Self also manifests as a human being; the source of life is the Self; the Self is not born and so does not die.

These are almost articles of faith in yogic philosophy. The yogi must tread cautiously here lest the practice becomes just another ideology, a catechism, or dogma. Yoga aims to liberate the mind prisoners, not to swap one intellectual cage for another.

A sleeping person realises life by sleeping through life itself. A person who is awake realises Supreme Life. A higher state of awareness opens the mind to other dimensions of being without doctrine or ideology.

As soon as transcendental experiences are considered factual truths, the mind is beset by dogma. Consciousness is never dogmatic. The author of the Avadhuta Gita wrote *Consciousness neither exists nor does not exist.*

The three habitual states of awareness, the waking, dream and deep sleep state are embedded in the three-dimensional world of time and space. The higher state of *turiya* is ultra-dimensional, beyond the causal world. Finally, in the fourth state, with an intellect sharpened by knowledge, a person can eventually experience the revelation of something indescribable that transcends everyday human experience. This is what is meant by self-realisation.

Exercise 8

Awareness of Higher Self

Be aware of the multiplicity of objects and things experienced in the waking state are anchored in the divided and partial reality. On the other hand, the senses define how the world is known, giving rise to the illusion that the world experienced through the senses is an individual experience.

Benefits

The goal of the Yogi is perfect unity with Higher Consciousness by seeing through the veil of a divided reality. Therein lies our potential and ultimate success in life.

HIGHER CONSCIOUSNESS

Cosmic intelligence permeates both sentient life forms and insentient objects, but only sentient creatures experience Consciousness. By sentient, we mean life forms such as humans, animals, insects, flowers, trees. But it does not end there. For example, a stone has no neuronal system to experience the world. However, a stone is still aware, a vibration in time and space, in the relative field.

The intelligence of Consciousness is claimed by the inner actor, or ego, and becomes human Consciousness. The intellect processes the changes in the relative field and registers them as experience., resulting in likes and dislikes. The mind claims ownership of Consciousness. The collective human mind claims ownership of all knowledge and the right to use this knowledge to exert dominium over all the beings, sentient or non-sentient. Livestock is eaten, fields ploughed for food, the earth drilled for oil, mountains ripped apart, the air polluted.

But Consciousness is not a mechanical process, nor is it individual or subject to belief. Awareness, ego, intellect, and mind are all formed by kundalini's power, which is not confined to our three-dimensional model of decoding intelligence in time and space. A sense of discrimination between what is useful and what is irrelevant is required. Vivek is the innate sense of discrimination, a faculty inherent to the mind.

Developing the ability to discriminate is one of the skills developed in Yoga. It is a vital skill to acquire if we are to achieve our personal goals.

The human mind is programmed to discriminate, making choices, between this and that, making choices, making decisions. So humans as a species with an acute sense of discrimination also mean the highest potential for self-realisation.

The power to discriminate between multiplicities of options is a fundamental faculty of the mind. Discrimination takes place before choosing, and this is where the opportunity to see past the seemingly mechanical process of making a choice presents itself. At the moment after desire arises, but before a choice is made, there is a window of opportunity to allow expanded awareness of a higher intellect. The environment in which higher Consciousness is the material world, *Prakriti*. Discrimination is the window from the material world into the dimension of opportunity and potential. From this dimension of possibility and potential, we reshape our reality.

The material field of existence covers more than the world experienced with the senses, mind or imagination. Using instruments and mathematical calculations, we have explored both the observable and unobservable universe.

Prakriti is both a formed reality and an unformed reality comprised of the world already in existence and the unmanifest world yet to become or imagined. To put it succinctly, Prakriti is the known and unknown world. The field of Prakriti has the power to give rise to all kinds of manifestations, and this is the basis of a world vision of multiplicity. It is a manifestation of pure Consciousness in the physical realm.

By enhancing our sense of discrimination, we manifest the opportunities and potential of Higher Consciousness into our lives.

Purusha is the formless force or spirit that permeates all. Prakriti and Purusha are two aspects of existence that the expanded mind can discriminate between with the faculty of *Vivek*.

Exercise 9

Awareness of Vivek

30 minutes

Be aware of how the whole universe appears to be coming into existence and going into a state of dissolution, just as bubbles of water appear and disappear in the ocean. The forms of plants and trees appear from light and in the end, disappear into light.

Be aware of the essential and non-essential, purposeful and purposeless.

Benefits:

You become aware of what aspects of your life are helpful and what is superfluous, resulting from habit and conditioning. As a result, you start to make better choices.

THE YOGA OF DEVOTION

The Yoga of Bhakti is a unity of love and devotion. Bhakti Yoga transcends the realm of the intellect and the ego-mind.

When the yogi has become united with that something that has no name, this is bhakti consciousness. Thus, Bhakti Yoga is performed by the minds or hearts that have fully expanded or attained their true nature.

The path of Bhakti Yoga exists for anyone who wishes to remove the mental sense of separation.

The sense of separation can be removed by recalling devotion, in any situation, at any place. Every thought and action are devoted to Supreme Consciousness.

The man or woman who has attained the state of Bhakti Yoga never thinks about separation because devotion dissolves that sense of the other.

Bhakti love is not the modern love of romance and rom-com movies. The romantic love between two people that we know today was absent from the Upanishads and Vedas. For the most part, Buddhism is silent on the concept of love as we understand it, talking instead of loving-kindness (Metta) and compassion (Karuna), which are both selfless. The *Kama Sutra* is a treatise of all aspects of desire in human relationships, but romantic love did not figure in this. The modern sense of personal, romantic love did not compute in an age when marriage was a commercial transaction.

Bhakti is the cosmic love that is eternal and all-pervasive. Bhakti Yoga reaches into and expands the inner cosmic heart of the human being. In the state of Bhakti, there is no difference between darkness and light, ignorance and knowledge, disciple and master, student and Guru, or Man and God.

In the heart of a yogi, devotion flows effortlessly like a river into the ocean of love. Devotion springs from meditation because love is union. Love cannot be divided. The Yoga Sutras describe Bhakti as devotion to a Higher Consciousness.

RADICAL MEDITATION

*The Yogi should imagine the heart to be a sublime
ocean of golden honey, with an island made of jewels.
The sand on the shore is made of gemstones. Kadamba
trees with abundant flowers on the ground. Bees buzz
and doves coo. He should prepare himself and visualise
a bejewelled pavilion radiating in his body.'*

The Gheranda Samhita

The sole purpose of meditation is to tear down the structures
of the mind. To achieve ground zero. The practice of
meditation is not a cosy affair with the tinkling of bells and
banging of gongs. It is not just about feeling calm and
peaceful. Meditation is a radical rewrite of the mind's
operating system.

An analogy is weightlifting. If you put pressure on the spine
rather than your muscles, you will end up harming yourself.
In meditation, you use the power of higher Consciousness,
not the mind. Meditating with the mind will just reinforce the
structures of personality.

*Meditation is radically different to any other human experience.
Along the path, you will find happiness and a renewed sense of*

purpose in your life. But there are no shortcuts and no half measures. Meditation is a total experience.

No method, no teacher

As soon as anyone tries to teach meditation, a system is created. A method is beneficial as much as a structure puts the mind at ease, but a system is still a system. And if a person believes in the system, they become a prisoner. Initially, a meditator may need a guide or a teacher who follows a method. Still, eventually, the method will naturally dissolve into something much freer flowing. Consciousness is not a system, although many people instinctively look for a technique with rules and regulations.

Through meditation, a person can experience the reality of a universe within and as the entire universe *without*. Divisions such as an inner or outer reality or within or without are experienced in the same reality-space. The sense of separation from higher Consciousness dissolves. Radical meditation opens an awareness of the true nature of inner and outer reality.

Thoughts are processes and expressions of energy that arise from a formless source, pure thought with no relatable experience. The mind is the mental field of expertise in which all this thought-creation happens. By allowing the active thinking process to slow down and quieten, the mind can gradually dissolve back into the source of all thinking. This formless thought is an unconditioned state of existence.

Radical meditation induces a state of mind that allows the meditator to directly experience higher Consciousness, revealing the immense potential of the visible phenomenal world. From prehistory to the most advanced theories of relativity and quantum physics, all philosophies of life and science derive inspiration from the same source. Every concept, economic, scientific, technological, astronomical, mystic, and spiritual, arises from this formless thought-reality.

Your future success will be a manifestation of this formless thought-reality. Your potential is the same to be realised in the present moment.

Meditation became more highly developed in India than anywhere else and spread globally. In India, yogis practised meditation with different ways of approaching the source of formless thought: Tantra, Jnana, Bhakti, Raja, Karma methodologies, all different in some respects but all transcendentally the same.

At the heart of the meditative experience is the realisation that every human being manifests energy. In its purest form, this energy is pure thought or Consciousness.

This energy is unchanging and is the essence of things that come and go in and out of existence. The crucial point is that this energy is in everything but is not involved. And this uninvolvement comes from the unchanging nature of source energy.

What does not change cannot be bound to the things that change.

Through meditation, a person realises that the thinking mind cannot make any accurate judgment on the nature of reality. However, human Consciousness has the inherent potential to be transformed into a more highly evolved thinking process, free from delusion. But it means adopting a radical approach to our meditation practice.

Meditation is often depicted as a panacea to all our misfortune and problems. The message is: meditate, and all our problems will miraculously disappear. It is facile to highlight the bright side of meditation and ignore the potential downside.

Psychological research and testimony have shown the value of meditation in reducing stress levels, deepening our meaning in life, reducing pain and making it easier to fall asleep. However, it is also essential for us to recognize the potential dangers that may arise during meditation. This is especially important for beginners. It is also vital for meditation and yoga teachers to be aware of these potential dangers. Their students may encounter similar challenges and need support.

There is no single "correct" way of meditation. We all have highly individual psychological profiles and have been subject to different conditioning. No one size fits all.

Some teachers and books claim that their meditation technique is the "right" way and even regard other methods as wrong. Fame, money, and ego are a toxic mix. One of the most beautiful things about meditation is that it can be practised in many ways and using many techniques. Flexibility and openness are essential, and the claim that there is only one effective way of meditation has limitations. Practising the wrong meditation technique can be a painful, even harmful experience; if you still feel unease after trying one meditation method for a while, you need to switch to another.

The most profound interaction you experience in meditation is the interaction with yourself. During introspection, you will be exposed to buried and suppressed emotions. For example, meditation may arouse deep anger, fear, or jealousy in you, making you very uncomfortable, though these emotions will gradually subside. However, suppose you don't know that meditation can resurrect these feelings and memories that have been long suppressed. In that case, the practitioner may avoid meditation altogether as a painful experience.

Some people experience moments of rapture and elation or visions of light and souls rising. Although this may be an experiential side effect of meditation, seeking this experience does not help. If you don't have the experience you want, you will feel frustrated.

Meditation is unpredictable, and the mind instinctively tries to control the chaos. Many beginners are simply unprepared for the downside.

The meditating Buddha has become an icon - the eyes closed, a serene expression, in the lotus posture. This iconic image is essentially an idealised characterisation of the historical Buddha with Greek sculptural influences, depicting meditation as a peaceful, calm, and deep connection with the physical and spiritual realms.

This is a highly stylized depiction of meditation. But unfortunately, the experience is not that simple.

Worries, nervous ticks, aches and pains and a myriad of thoughts may disturb the mind. Some people have high expectations of immediate epiphany. Some experience an initial release of stress and worry, which induces an endorphin rush. The intellect and the senses create a world, and the ego clings to its existence in the waking state. With practice, the meditator can disassociate self-identity from mental activity

You may have your own expectations for meditation: sitting still for a long time, calm and not angry after reflection; the list is long. We are human beings, so it is sometimes difficult to sit down and meditate or feel relaxed in our skins. This is entirely natural.

It is not uncommon to experience intense uplifts of spirit during meditation when our hearts begin to truly open to the cosmos. Although this experience is usually pleasant and even euphoric, it can sometimes become antagonistic or even scary. Sometimes meditative experiences can be so intense and disturbing that people give up meditation altogether. Fortunately, when we understand what triggers these intense experiences, we can be prepared to deal with them. Whether it's euphoria, fear, or something in between, these experiences happen in the same way.

The process of what we usually call thinking is to make the same decisions in a loop. When our normal thought process cycle is slowed in meditation, our memories, beliefs and emotions are not filtered by our thoughts. Unfettered psychological and emotional trauma rise from the subconscious. These intense, unfiltered experiences may provoke an extreme reaction with a psychological fight or flight response.

> *There are many ways to deal with negative or disturbing meditation experiences.*
> *We can change our meditation and instead use techniques that attract pleasant thoughts. For example, one can meditate by looking at a candle or a flower or adopt a mantra for reassurance. In time, the practice becomes familiar and less threatening.*

Meditation is a long-term journey that can heal and nourish, but it can be a lonely experience. If someone is struggling and seeking help, meditation may not provide the support they hope for. They may need to see a therapist to feel heard and understood.

When we deal with our unpleasant experiences in meditation practice, we need to learn to withdraw from the experiences. Otherwise, the loop processing of random thoughts can be unbearable

These experiences come from our own memories, emotions, and beliefs. Therefore, it is crucial to develop non-attachment to our past experiences.

Non-attachment is one of the pillars of meditation. This entails stepping back from our feelings to acknowledge the transitory nature of mental activity. This quality of non-attachment is paramount because it helps us realise thoughts and feelings are manifestations of a far greater consciousness – if only we can detach ourselves from identifying with them

However, this kind of non-attachment does not mean avoiding, suppressing, or disregarding something. We should not disengage from the people and activities we like and love, nor should we become passive or inactive. Non-attachment only requires us to revaluate how we relate to the external world and redefine our relationship with our self-identity.

It is easy to fall into the trap of becoming a good person for practising meditation, somehow made worthy and virtuous, or worse still, superior to other people. Undoubtedly, meditation does sharpen the mind, and with intense practice, higher consciousness skills develop. However, to claim these as ours is a misstep. Higher consciousness has no ego and claims nothing.

desire (v.)
early 13c., from Old French desirrer (12c.) "wish, desire, long for," from Latin desiderare "long for, wish for; demand, expect," original sense perhaps "await what the stars will bring," from the phrase de sidere "from the stars.

Desire is the driving force of human activity. When we desire to do better in life, we push ourselves out of our comfort zone. Ambition to succeed is healthy and natural, and desire is the engine of our aspirations and purpose, the force that propels us forward. Therefore, desire in moderation is to be acknowledged as part of your life experience. Even better, desire is the force that gets us on the path of Yoga.

The Kama[2] Sutra analyses the influence of desire in human affairs, corresponding to the Greek concept of Eros. God moves through the material world as Kama or Eros.

Let's talk about sex

Shakti power is the feminine power of the cosmos, forever present in the material world as a creative force. Shakti power moves the show of creation. However, neither the male nor female forces of the cosmos can exist in isolation. *Prakriti Laya* is the merging of the brute male force of Prakriti and the

---

[2] *Kama is desire, not to be confused with karma, action.*

creative feminine energy of Shakti. The act of sex with *Prakti Laya* in mind is a form of worship of Shakti.

In the Buddhist teachings, Kama Sava, sensual desire, is considered as unskillful use of the mind. Kama is considered as both desire and the sensual pleasure associated with those actions.

With desire often comes guilt. There is no natural equivalent Sanskrit word for shame, no term that encapsulates the transgression of a moral code. Guilt to be absolved, as in the Christian tradition, does not figure in Yoga. However, when directed towards a noble purpose, kama is positive.

Some Indian temples and monuments like the Khajuraho or Sun Temple of Konark are extreme in depicting sexual activity, all varieties of sexual positions, even bestiality. The extreme images on the Indian temples reflect the power of unfiltered desire in the human imagination.

From desire comes the joy of achievement. Bliss - *Ananda* - is a word that comes loaded with associations, suggesting a supreme pleasure in a divine realm, in mystic rapture, riding a flow of endorphins and a joy that transcends the world.

In Sanskrit, bliss is associated with *sat* and *chit*, pure bliss and consciousness. Bliss is the apex of all human pleasure, the joy that connects into a vastly wider and deeper cosmic system. The mind travels into the mystic and disassociates itself from the body, thereby liberating the ego and sense of self-identity. On achieving that liberation, mental bliss is experienced.

Sat chit ananda is a powerful mantra to keep in mind when meditating, meaning Pure Consciousness and Bliss.

Exercise 10

Awareness of Higher Consciousness

Meditating with awareness of higher consciousness establishes in you a sense of potential greatness wherever you go or whatever you do. You see your path clearly and the direction that you are travelling in. You feel no need to alter or change because just by being aware of the power of a higher consciousness in your life sets you right. Just like water finds its level, so too will you find your balance.

Do not dwell on thoughts or revelations or insights. And don't try to remember or claim. Simply be aware and the rest will follow.

Benefits

In time you will be more confident in your choices and will cease to be influenced by events over which you have no control. Your insight into the workings of the world increases. You stay engaged but without attachment to dreams and fantasies on what might be. You are more focused.

THE YOGA OF PRANAYAMA

Pranayama is a yoga exercise that is invariably overlooked in favour of the asanas. But pranayama is an integral part of yoga, and its health benefits may even exceed those of the postural movements. Moreover, pranayama practice is undoubtedly more relevant post covid for those who contracted the virus and have suffered lung damage and impairment to their respiratory system.

Furthermore, studies have shown that pranayama breathing exercises are beneficial for people suffering from a wide range of ailments, from endometriosis, to swollen prostate, sleep apnoea, asthma, and acid reflux, as well as being a factor in breaking down visceral fat. Pranayama improves the flow of kundalini in the body and increases the flow of oxygen to the brain.

Another benefit of this ancient exercise is that it balances the brain, distributing energy to both the left and right sides of the brain. This aids both physical and mental poise.

Improved lung capacity also means that the asanas can be practised without huffing, puffing, or feeling dizzy.

Prana is breath. *Yama* is a suspension. *Pranayama* - the practice of breath control -regulates the flow of *kundalini* in the body. Pranayama is a gentle form of Yoga and is one of the eight 'limbs' of Yoga in the Sutras of Patanjali, a manual of meditative Yoga.

Most schools of Yoga include pranayama as a core element of teacher training. In the Yoga Sutras, pranayama is said to remove the veil that covers the light of the mind., preparing the mind for meditation.

Pranayama is a gentle exercise. Add a mantra to the exercise, and the results can be astounding. A mantra is a hybrid Sanskrit term from *man* -mind – and *tra* – tool, which essentially means a tool for cleansing the mind.

Many teachers on YouTube encourage strenuous breathing and extended retention of breath. These are not useful and can even be dangerous because holding the breath for too long can create capillary damage to the brain. Overstraining the abdomen can inflame the lining of the stomach.

These exercises are to be done seated on a sofa or cross-legged in the half-lotus position. In all pranayama exercises, the idea is to draw energy from the base of spine upwards by bringing the abdomen in and up. Then just release the stomach muscles to a relaxed position.

For people with hernias, it is very important to go gently.

Over time, core muscles are strengthened. Posture improves and the belly becomes less bloated and extended – provided a healthy lifestyle is maintained with regular yoga asanas and a good eating regime.

There are three principal exercises that are performed in a specific order for maximum benefit.

1: Kapalbhati

(Pronounced kap - al – barty)

The practice of *pranayama* begins with the plexus exercise which, strengthens the pelvic muscles, rejuvenates the prostate in men and the uterus in women and cleans the intestines of excess wind.

The plexus focused exercises done for fifteen minutes in the morning and in the evening opens a connection to the fire energy in the body. In pranayama exercises, breathing becomes a conscious process that enables the body to function in a state of balance.

Pranayama Exercise 1

Imagine a ball of light at the base of the spine or in the lower abdomen. You expel air from your nose, drawing the breath up from this ball of light, causing the muscles in your solar plexus to pull your stomach in. If you have blocked sinuses, you can expel air from the mouth for the same effect.

Finish by expelling the air and holding your breath for between 10 and 30 seconds, or for as long as it feels comfortable.

Kapalbhati be done for between five and ten minutes.

Benefits: *The Kapalbhati exercise stimulates the upward flow of energy through the spine into the chest. The muscles and nerves in the d pelvic area are stretched and strengthened, flattening the flat stomach*

2: Anulom Vilom

(Pronounced anu-lom vi-lom)
Breathing through alternate nostrils.

The exercise of breathing in through alternate nostrils calms the waves of mental energy.

The exercise should not be done too vigorously lest it disturbs the nervous system. At the end of a pranayama session, the mind and body will feel energised but peaceful too.

You close the left nostril with your thumb, then breathe in through your right nostril, drawing the breath up from the bottom of your lungs.

Hold for a few seconds, without straining.

Then simultaneously close your right nostril with your middle finger and lift your finger from your left nostril, expelling the air from through your left nostril.

Then switch to the other side. After a few seconds, breath in through your left nostril, hold, then simultaneously close your left nostril with your thumb finger and lift your finger from your right nostril, expelling the air from through your right nostril.

How hard and long you hold is up to you. Do not overdo it, especially at first. Otherwise, you may feel dizzy.

Avoid Anulom Vilom if you have blocked sinuses.

Pranayama Exercise 2

Do Anulom Vilom for between five and ten minutes as above.

Benefits: This exercise draws the breath from the lower lungs to the top, expelling stale air and stimulating the pulmonary alveoli. These are air sacs or air space, millions of hollow cup-shaped cavities in the lungs where oxygen is exchanged for carbon dioxide. People with respiratory problems after a severe flu infection or Covid, resulting from pollution or a childhood whooping cough, can benefit from the stimulation and opening of the alveoli.

An additional benefit is balancing the oscillating electrical voltages in the brain and calming the brain cycles to the Alpha state.

3: Bhastrika

(Pronounced ba-stri-ka)

This simple exercise involves drawing breath from the lower lungs and expelling with slight force from the nostrils. Then change from the nostrils to expelling air from the mouth.

To gauge the force involved, put a sheet of paper in front of your nose or mouth. The sheet should move slightly. If it bends, you are probably overexerting yourself.

Pranayama Exercise 3

Bhastrika for between five and ten minutes as above.

Benefits:

Bhastrika opens the lungs and sinuses, strengthening air flows. Energy is drawn up from the spine, improving posture. In the yogic, this exercise opens the heart chakra or Anahata in its original Sanskrit name, thereby engendering compassion, love, and beauty. Driven by the principles of transformation and integration, the fourth energy centre is said to bridge earthly and spiritual aspirations.

Bhastrika can be done with eyes closed or open. In both cases, Beta waves in the brain become focused on a single point without loop processing thoughts. Abstract opportunities materialise. When done with the eyes open and focussed on one object – for example, a leaf, a candle or anything in your vision line- it increases peripheral vision awareness. This enhances spatial awareness and a sense of balance.

The benefits of pranayama are not measured in short-term improvements, unlike hatha postural yoga, which helps bodies become flexible relatively quickly. Pranayama will help lung function after a few months' practice. After six months, the results are remarkable. Pranayama is most beneficial when it becomes a lifestyle, half an hour to forty-five minutes daily, followed by fifteen minutes of meditation.

The exercises lead naturally into a state of calm mind from which meditation flows naturally. With the addition of a mantra, the loop of thoughts that arise in meditation gets resolved. Mantras are designed to resonate with a quiet mind, especially when the body's energy flows are balanced. Opening the voice is a great way to start or end the day.

Pranayama is also suitable for people who cannot do Yoga due to a physical disability, such as a bad back or an arthritic hip, but who nevertheless wish to adopt a Yogic lifestyle. In addition, many people who do not enjoy the practice of Yoga asanas regularly practise pranayama.

MAYA -ILLUSION

Magic is a real force in the world. How we harness this magic is the key to maximizing potential and opportunity.

Maya is the deceptive phenomenon of illusion. It is an elemental force that gives rise to the appearance of things. Maya and myth combine to create the world according to the mind. Traditionally Maya is a feminine shakti power. Maya was the name of the Buddha's mother. Mary (Maya) is the name of the mother of Jesus Christ.

Maya is Magic, the force of nature manifested as a perceptual reality experienced through the senses. The mechanism of Maya is like a great magician who deceives us into seeing what is not there, thereby diverting our attention from what is happening.

With meditation and pranayama, we develop the awareness to see what is really happening.

The root of Maya is the Sanskrit verb *man-* or "to think", implying that we think the world into existence. In the early days of humanity, the Vedic mystics identified an elusive and magical power that turns ideas into our physical reality. The word magic derives from Maya. The Magus is the male personification of Maya.

The purpose of Maya is to trick us by hijacking consciousness and creating bondage to the empirical world. When the mind meets consciousness, Maya intervenes, giving rise to an illusory world of competing shapes, forms and ideas.

Maya is a psychological conditioning that breaks reality down into single packets of information, making it easier for the brain to process the data flow. But the force of Maya protects as well as deceives. Without the illusion of Maya, consciousness would be experienced as chaos.

Patanjali in the Yoga Sutras gives a detailed breakdown of how to neutralise the force of illusion. By turning attention from the external world inwards to the mind, where Maya operates, the mechanics of illusion become evident. That world comes in seed form, and seeds grow and take shape. That form is our child, born of magic, the child of Maya, our original space.

The greatest trick that Maya pulled is getting humanity to believe that the world exists. The origin of this illusion stems from the separation between consciousness and causal reality, the realm of Maya. Thus, we experience the world as Maya, as an illusion, not as Higher Consciousness.

Exercise 11

:45

Awareness of Maya

Be aware the potential of Higher Consciousness in your life. Notice the changing nature of everything and the force of Maya which gives it a sense of permanency. You are moving through time and space. Just be aware of change and how everything seems so fixed and permanent. Whereas you are not the same person you were a minute ago, moving at the speed of light in an unimaginably large universe. Be open to change. The changing flux of reality is the source of your potential.

Benefits.

This exercise frees you from attachment to a fixed identity of who you are, allowing you to establish an identity that you choose, not the one that was imposed on you by your social conditioning and circumstances. With a renewed sense of identity, potential unfolds.

Maya

I heard that at one time the Buddha was dwelling near Savatthi, in Jeta's Wood, at Anathapindika's monastery. The Gracious One was inspiring his audience with a Dhamma talk about enlightenment. Those monks all were listening attentively to the Buddha. The Gracious One uttered this mind-blowing utterance:
"There is a sphere, monks, where there is no earth, no water, no fire, no air, no sphere of infinite space, no sphere of infinite consciousness, no sphere of nothingness, no sphere of neither perception nor non-perception, not this world, no world beyond, neither Moon nor Sun.
There, monks, I say there is undoubtedly no coming, no going, no persisting, and no passing away, no rebirth. It is uninvolved, unmoving, without an object. This is the end of unhappiness."
The Buddha's Third Discourse on Nibbana

BELIEF, TRUST AND CONFIDENCE

The Middle English word *'beleven'* originally meant 'to love'. And the Latin word credo is derived from the phrase *'cor do'* – I give my heart. So to transcend the present moment, you have to surrender what you believe to be true. You have to offer your heart.

The Buddha was an Indian guru whose teachings emerged from the mystical Vedas. Don't believe in anything that I tell you, he said. Put my words to the test, and then believe in yourself.

Buddhism did not embrace the concept of cosmic consciousness but instead is centred on the idea of a non-self, stating that there is no eternal, unchanging essence. There is nothing to believe in because the truth is relative to experience. Later Buddhist scriptures, the Mahayana, introduce the concept of the sunyata, a void, a state devoid of attributes.

Buddhism is neither atheistic nor religious.

"I do not care to know your various theories about God. What is the use of discussing all the subtle doctrines about the soul? Do good and be good. And this will take you to freedom and to whatever truth there is." The Buddha

Belief, Trust and Confidence

This ambiguity can be troublesome for those of us who need certainties to believe in.

Belief systems comprise a conditioned set of ideas, arrangements, notions, ideology, and concepts. Thus, for example, in the Avadhuta Gita, a song-poem of extreme Advaita, it is written:

Pure consciousness is free from any sense of duality, which is mental. Instead, pure consciousness is Oneness, all-permeating. It has no attributes, good or bad, right, or wrong, which are all imagination.

Beliefs are part of a value system. Therefore, the yogi strenuously cultivates non-attachment even to personal beliefs.

The teachings of Yoga have broken down the duality of world vision into a super good consciousness that transcends belief systems, not only those of religion but also of science. All differences between belief systems are purely conceptual. If those beliefs get cemented or written in stone, they become exclusive and tribal. Exclusivity leads to conflict.

Krishna told Arjuna on the eve of the big battle: When you believe you are the one doing the killing; you become the victim of a concept. Even enlightenment is a concept. To know God, you have to be free of all attachments.

There is an Indian saying: *painting legs on a snake won't make it walk*. So you cannot believe your way to enlightenment.

All truths are false and true simultaneously, despite what reason and evidence would have us believe. But we cannot live like this. Otherwise, there would be chaos. So truth both exists at a practical level, the world that we see and feel. And also at a transcendental level. Unfortunately, however, so many of our activities in our waking life are conditioned by our belief systems. As a result, we limit our potential and close the door of opportunity.

Our lives seem to be a succession of disconnected events. We use a platform to build our world and our lives on. The more we see, touch and feel, the more robust this platform becomes. We create an identity for ourselves, like a coat hanger on which we hang our existence. We look into a mirror, and the mirror confirms the image that we have of ourselves. We experience our past through memory and use the experience of imperceptible changes to interpret the sensory data of the present moment. And then, we create scenarios for the future. We become the author and main protagonist of a movie, a succession of frames, and imagine our world into existence.

We need to be aware of how our belief systems and ideologies are limiting the scope of our potential. Of course, we need structure and values and moral codes. But we need to be aware of how these codes and systems impact us and if they are impositions, restricting our ability to choose.

Exercise 12

:55

Awareness of Beliefs

Be aware that you are a person with beliefs and a belief system. Do not analyse what you believe in or the beliefs of people you know – your children or parents perhaps. It is sufficient to be aware that believing in something is an aspect of human conditioning. People believe in things others flatly reject. One person's lie is another person's truth. Is the earth flat or round?

Simply be aware that you probably have deeply held beliefs. To believe is to be human. Rejoice in your ability to believe, but neither accept nor challenge.

Benefits

Increased awareness of the different psychological structures that makes us human opens potentiality.

Your beliefs are safe because meditation is not about believing. Instead, once you have transcended the ordinary mind, your beliefs become self-evident truths.

PART 2

Scripts to live by

THE YOGA SUTRAS OF PATANJALI

1: The Path to Transforming your life

Yoga is the transcendental state of peace and stillness where consciousness flows freely. In this state of peace and serenity, our mind reflects higher consciousness. As a result, we become charismatic, and people are attracted to our presence and drawn to our radiance.

When not in this transcendental state of stillness, our mind is caught up in the stream of relative consciousness, constantly loop processing thoughts. We self-limit our potential.

We take what we believe to be true from direct observation, logically deducing it to be accurate or hearing it from a confirmed authority. The definition of delusion is creating an idea of something that is not real and then taking this to be true.

Abstract or conceptualised knowledge originates from experiences. Memory draws on a pool of accumulated past mental impressions to create an idea of something we take to be authentic.

Not becoming entangled in loop processing of thoughts requires practice and detachment. This calls for a sustained effort to remain in a state of peace and stillness. With skill and dedication, this practice becomes progressively grounded.

A sense of detachment is experienced when the mind does not react to physical or intellectual sensory data. Finally, the highest level of objectivity is experienced when the mind is utterly free of reactions to the stream of consciousness. This is the purest state of awareness.

Pleasant thoughts, insight, a sense of happiness and joy arise.

With regular and enthusiastic practice, our mind becomes calm and still, and mental activity subsides, leaving only the imprint of previous karma. These karmas leave the body on death and are dissolved into nature, passing from one state of existence into another

Practice

Trust, enthusiasm, focus, the practice of meditation and the development of wisdom leads to enlightenment. Those who fully embrace the spiritual practice will surely experience self-fulfilment. How long this takes depends on our effort and commitment.

Pure Consciousness is unconditioned and unaffected by anything that goes on. It is pure intelligence, never moved by the workings of the world.

Pure Consciousness is also beyond the confines of space and time and existed before the creation of the universe.

Repeating a mantra such as Om clears the mind of attachments. The direction of the mind then turns inwards, with increasing clarity.

Ill-health, disinterest, lack of attention and resolve, procrastination, self-doubt, and pessimism are sources of negative energy which prevent progress. When the mind is stirred up by such negative energy flows, anxiety or depression ensues. As a result, sitting and breathing comfortably may become difficult.

There are many techniques to prevent the mind from becoming distracted during practice.

One calming technique is to develop feelings of warmth and compassion for other people, share their joy and successes, and develop equanimity.

Another calming technique is to observe the breath as it rises and falls, being aware of sensations.

Circumstances and situations which uplift the spirit should be cultivated. Hostile environments should be avoided.

As the mind becomes still in meditation, the meditator enters a state of quiet contemplation. The workings of the mind become transparent, and reality is seen clearly, without any super-imposition of prejudices.

When this transparent mind is still defined by thoughts and concepts, this is *reactive meditation*. The thinking process still leaves traces or impressions that germinate into feeling, ideas and karma.

This state of detachment then evolves into a more subtle meditation. The mind ceases to identify with thoughts, mental associations or memories.

Meditation on the essence of objects can spark off reactions in the mind. However, with practice, the mind can stay free of all associative activity, without reacting, in a state of awareness.

The essence of objects can then be seen as originating in formless consciousness.

In the highest state of meditation, the nature of the self is evident.

The knowledge that arises from the highest state of meditation is all-embracing.

This knowledge is unlike any insight into human existence or moments of relative expertise. It is the knowledge that sees clearly and simultaneously both the transient world of conditioned existence and the unconditioned realm of transcendental reality

In this transcendental state of mind, there are no fresh impulses to awaken karma. Instead, these remain dormant and eventually fade back into non-existence.

Eventually, no karmas arise in the perfectly still mind, and no karmas past, present or future. Therefore, we are open to opportunities without prejudice.

2: The Means to reach your potential

The Yoga of action (*kriya yoga*) has three components: discipline and training, self-study, and dedication to pure consciousness.

We practice yoga to weaken negative impulses and to induce a state of contemplation into the potential of our existence

There are five impediments to practice:

Not seeing the true nature of things.

Individuality or ego-based reactions.

Addictions

Avoidance

A subconscious fear of death.

Not seeing things clearly is the root cause of psychological impediments. Some people feel they can overcome such obstacles, while others feel overwhelmed and hopeless.

Avidya is the phenomenon of failing to see the transient nature of all the mental and physical things.

We mistake transcendental consciousness for the intellectual faculty of the individual mind.

Attachment is, simply put, a mental reaction to the memory of pleasurable experiences.

Aversion arises when consciousness is associated with an unpleasant experience.

Fear of death is instinctive, as is the desire to cling to life.

Seeing how the world's personal experience is conditioned by the senses will help reduce unpleasant experiences.

In meditation, the mind's instinctive reaction to the waves of individual consciousness is subdued.

The mind is a repository of latent impressions that can be awoken in this lifetime or possibly in another.

If the root cause of these karmas is not seen clearly, they will seed new reactions and spark interactions with existing karma.

The degree of happiness or sorrow is determined by how these latent karmas have been conditioned.

A yogi understands the unsatisfactory nature of existence and all phenomena. The constantly evolving nature of our physical reality affects our moods and emotional states.

Pain, suffering and sorrow (dukkha) yet to be experienced can be avoided. The preventable cause of future pain, suffering, and grief is associating ourselves with the things experienced. In this way, a conceptual sense of self is created, which is open to unpleasant experiences. We make ourselves miserable.

However, this phenomenal world experienced through the senses is the only platform that we have at our disposal to realise our potential. And it is in this world that opportunities arise

We experience the phenomenal world as both evident and unobvious, gross and subtle. These qualities are manifested from relative consciousness, which is a potential form of pure consciousness. Therefore, the yogi sees the whole world as a field of possible opportunity.

Pure consciousness exists of itself, undivided, unchanging. It is experienced in mind through the senses and mental activity.

The purpose of relative human consciousness, therefore, is to reveal an absolute higher consciousness.

When the phenomenal world is experienced as pure consciousness, there is no sense of division.

The faculty of associating a sense of self with the manifestation of consciousness is the potential for personal development.

However, we need to clearly understand that the association of our self-identity with things and ideas is not an authentic experience of pure consciousness. Otherwise, we are not open to our full potential as human beings.

The Yogi develops the skill to recognise that self-identity changes over time.

There is relative human consciousness and higher transcendental consciousness.

The ability to discriminate between relative and transcendental consciousness is innate.

By enthusiastically practising yoga, the fog of confusion dissolves and the light of potential shines bright

Ashtanga Yoga

The components of *ashtanga* yoga are restraint in thought and actions, mental cleansing, correct posture, pranayama, concentration, meditative contemplation and transcendence.

The five basic precepts are non-violence, living in truth, not stealing, devotion to higher consciousness and non-attachment to the senses.

The five practices of self-improvement are: attention to health, the development of equanimity, self-discipline, self-study, and awareness of higher consciousness.

Negative impulses can be balanced by positive mental activity.

Negative thoughts and ill will towards our fellow beings generate more negativity and are reciprocal.

A person who displays benevolence reduces hostility in others.

A person who deals only in truth will meet only truthful consequences.

By not taking what belongs to others, a person obtains much more in return.

By not wasting energy, vitality is increased.

By not clinging to the sensual world, the door to a far greater reality is opened.

By keeping the body in shape, physical discomfort and distractions can be avoided.

A healthy body and mind induce clarity of thought, contentment, powers of concentration, mastery of the senses and expansion of the mind.

Contentment expands to unlimited joy.

Eventually, the aesthetic lifestyle brings about mental clarity, leading to mastery over the senses and mind.

Self-study opens the mind to our potential as human beings.

By surrendering to pure consciousness, a state of complete absorption into meditation is reached.

Meditation posture should be comfortable, steady and stable.

When the body is perfectly relaxed and loose, the mind can better focus on the eternal source of conditioned phenomena.

The mind becomes free of dualities and the existential anxiety of living in a polarised world.

With perfect posture, the flow of breath becomes steady.

The Yogi practices awareness of breath (*prana*).

The breath is boundless energy operating on both the internal and external fields of reality.

With the breath still, the fog of confusion lifts and the natural radiance of the mind can shine brightly.

The mind is now prepared for meditation.

As the senses and mind withdraw from the external world and turn inwards, a process of interiorisation (*Pratyahara*) is initiated.

At this point, the mind and senses are prepared to connect with Pure Consciousness in meditation.

3: Higher Consciousness

Focusing on a single object, shape, form, or thought is a one-pointed concentration.

The meditating mind is absorbed in attention on that single object. This is called Dhyana or the Zen state of meditation.

The mind is fixed on a single object, and there is no sense of that object being something separate.

The mind gradually becomes more finely attuned to this process.

However, even at this stage of meditation, the mind leaves traces and its mark on the phenomenal world. Therefore, it is not free from the influence of karma.

The mental activity becomes more still, as active brain patterns respond to meditative consciousness's calming effect and tranquil quality.

This sense of calm and peace penetrates the subconscious, which in turn calms the conscious mind.

The mind is then less influenced by the changing facets of reality and moves towards a single point of consciousness.

When focused on a single point of consciousness, the mind rides the rise and fall of the waves of perception.

Likewise, the mind's conception of time and space is transformed.

Change

Everything in the universe is changing, or has changed, or will change, but in each change, there is an unmanifest and unseen constant that permeates everything

Change comes to pass when consciousness is conditioned by the flow of events.

By meditating on changes in shape and form over time, one develops insight into the past, present, and future.

Likewise, in meditation, awareness of how the mind processes words, their meaning and the ideas conveyed leads to insight into the very nature of language.

Meditation on deep memories and latent karma opens the mind to the knowledge of previous and future lifespans

Meditating on another person brings you closer to that person's mind and thoughts.

In meditating deeply on the nature of the body, all sense of being a separate entity dissolves, and the physical body merges with the interconnected web of manifest existence.

Likewise, the senses of sight, hearing, taste, smell, and touch are muted.

The subsequent revelation of potential may be sudden or slow to evolve. However, with resolute practice, deep insight into the nature of the world is developed.

Meditating deeply on love and kindness, compassion, joy in the success of others, and equanimity, we become invigorated with positive energy.

Whatever we put our mind to, we acquire those powers.

The light of higher knowledge sheds light on the minutiae of the physical world.

Our inner light also reveals the universe.

We come to know the working of the moon and stars.

We see the movements of the galaxies and universes.

We come to know the workings of the body.

We come to understand thirst and hunger.

We understand the workings of the mind.

We may come to know the wisdom of previous Yoga masters.

We may experience a brief insight into cosmic intelligence.

Focusing on the mind, insight into subtlest aspects of human behaviour grows.

However, even in the most enlightened minds, it is possible to confuse the subtlest aspects of human consciousness with absolute and pure consciousness. Focused and engaged meditation on both can open insight into undifferentiated consciousness.

With this insight into the transcendental mind, the powers of the senses are enhanced.

Although these powers are biproducts of the meditative process. They are considered distractions, to be neither avoided nor exploited, merely observed.

In following the flow of consciousness through the mind, it is possible to project consciousness into the physical space of another body.

By meditating on the rising nature of the energy within the body, we can reduce the limitations of gravity and become lighter.

By meditating upon the sense of hearing, we learn to appreciate music.

We lose weight by intense contemplation on the essence of lightness in physical objects.

When our consciousness is uninvolved with the passing flow of external events, we are connected to pure consciousness.

All things have five core components: what they are made of; their appearance, how we define them, how they came into being; their intended use and purpose. By meditating upon these five facets, one gains mastery over them.

With mastery over the core elements of things, we will transcend the body's limitations.

With deep meditation comes a deep understanding of the human mind and senses.

With detachment from association with the phenomenal world comes quickness of thought and the ability to see the origin of all things.

When a person can distinguish this highly evolved and rarefied state of fine human intelligence from absolute and uninvolved consciousness, one knows the nature of all conditioned things.

When even attachment to this supreme knowledge is broken, then a person is truly one with the world, free of hindrances and causality

However, we should be wary of taking pride in what we achieve because the ego will identify with the conditioned world at the slightest attachment to achievement.

Remaining in deep meditation on the passage of time, the light of pure consciousness shines eternally on all conditioned things

Duality and non-duality are then known to be as one, both relative and absolute.

One sees opportunity in all things.

One sees the undifferentiated light of consciousness shining in all things and dimensions of the material world, past, present, and future.

Self-fulfilment

Some people are naturally inclined to enter a state of contemplation. Herbs and drugs can calm the mind. Learning from books can help. Only meditation, however, leads to self-fulfilment.

Coming into being as a form and leaving this material form is a conditioned and co-dependent process.

It is the nature of the world to change, as is to react to the changing nature of the world.

The development of ego-based identity results from reactions to the waves of pure consciousness that get claimed as ours.

The continuous stream of consciousness generates countless reactions, yet we feel that this is just one experience.

Once we identify our self-identity with higher consciousness, our mind ceases to react and consolidate karma.

When the dualistic activity of cause and effect comes to an end, the mind ceases endlessly react to stimuli.

The past and future are just latent forms of the same reality, unmanifest permutations of the one experience.

The consciousness that is experiencing the world is unchanging and unaffected by what is known.

The mind, therefore, does not experience anything; it is just an experience of universal consciousness.

The mind can then achieve its potential, which is to experience both the world and consciousness simultaneously.

Like all conditioned things in this world, the mind has but one aim: to respond to consciousness.

As soon as a person can distinguish between the world as experienced by the mind and the world as experienced by pure consciousness, the ego melts away.

The mind is now conditioned by pure consciousness and moves in all aspects and activities towards release from the limitations of the phenomenal world.

Karma buried in the recess of the subconscious rises into light of current experience, where the meditating mind steers them into the light of consciousness,

At the highest point of mind intelligence, where consciousness flows between the field of relative reality and true reality, opportunities arise.

This enlightenment extinguishes the root of doubt and self-limitations.

With no superimpositions to dull the light of pure consciousness, insight into reality is boundless.

At this point, the mind has achieved its true potential.

Reality is experienced clearly as a succession of micro-phenomena in fractions of time, changing in four-dimensional spacetime

You witness the rising of each moment and transformation of reality yet are unmoved and uninvolved. Your spirit travels beyond until nothing else exists but existence alone. Herein lies self-fulfilment.

THE AVADHUTA GITA

Break things and move fast

The Avadhuta Gita is a work of extreme mysticism at the far end of reason and logic and the confines of the mind. It can be an unsettling read as the author, the legendary mystic Dattatreya, challenges every preconception that we have about the nature of our existence. Nothing is real — neither birth nor death, neither reality nor illusion, neither is nor is not. He leaves us nothing to hold onto, sweeping away everything we use to create our sense of existence and reality. He tells us the human condition is naturally free, in a state of Oneness.

The Avadhuta is an extreme idealist who rejects materialism. I am not a psychophysical organism. What am I then? The intellect can only make assumptions. Science will never be able to provide a satisfactory answer, he says — circumstances condition experience. In a world where everything conditions something else, our sense of identity is inevitably a collage of events we have no control over.

The Avadhuta takes back control by rejecting the validity of the physical world. Nothing happens because the 'you' that experiences the word is a fictional creation constructed from an imperceptible succession of receptive and responsive processes. You are as real as Micky Mouse. You write the script and direct your movie, creating a fascinating world of sound and colour. Life is good - until it isn't good anymore, and where to turn then? You have surrendered control to the world that you have created.

The Avadhuta Gita teaches us that to break free from our conditioned lives and fulfil our potential, we must be radical and disrupt our comfortable routines.

It is not the wandering the world in raggedy clothes that define the Avadhuta. Nor the lack of possessions and the disregard for social conventions. Nor the rejection of nationality and status, and self-identity. These are all irrelevant. The Avadhuta is pure consciousness, unidentified with any aspect of material existence, merely energy, moving through space, absolutely free.

The term consciousness itself is ambiguous. The Avadhuta talks of consciousness, God and Brahman as merely concepts, evoking an awareness of a pre-conceptual state of existence. In other words, before God became an idea in human consciousness

Consciousness in the Avadhuta Gita is not relative but absolute, the formless being from which the material world evolved, present but identified to every aspect of our reality.

The most challenging aspect of the Avadhuta Gita is the insistence that all reality, the entire human experience, is an illusion. That the only truth is the absolute state of perfection, Brahman.

This extreme take on the illusory nature of reality is not easy to digest. However, the Avadhuta Gita was intended for advanced students trained in the fundamentals of the different schools of Indian philosophy. These yogis had studied the Bhagavad Gita, the Vedas, the Upanishads, the Yoga Sutras and the Shrutis intensely and were prepared to go right to the edge of reason, to a dissolution of all conceptual knowledge.

Only a transcended state of mind can experience a state of abstract reality. To convey the totality of the experience is beyond the power of the intellect to grasp.

THE SONG OF THE MYSTIC WANDERER
BY THE SAGE DATTATREYA
WRITTEN ABOUT 6TH CENTURY CE

Many are those who hear the voice of God, but few choose to open their minds to the one reality that permeates our lives, the truth of our original space, our eternal and immortal self, undivided consciousness. I see the world from this timeless and full reality and understand the world to be a mirage. It is a place of wonder which I know is not real.

This world is not me, but my reality is the world. I am the reality that is conscious in all aspects of the world. My reality is undivided, always mindful, alive, or dead.

The nature of this reality is free, and my belief in the free spirit is unwavering and constant.

Terms such as good or bad or right and wrong are none of my concern because such concepts are divisive. I am not affected by either the doing or the results of actions. There is nothing more to gain and nothing less to lose. The idea that there being something to add or take away from my reality is a delusion.

My ordinary mind cannot conceive of undivided consciousness. Nothing is obvious or unobvious, seen or hidden, because the very act of seeing requires something else to be seen. In contrast, the underlying reality of existence can never be seen because it is never anything else. A thing is of itself and shines in everything.

There is no other thing. There is no day or night, no questions or answers. Even in meditation, this reality is undivided. You cannot meditate upon consciousness as if it were just another aspect of your experience and expect to get a result. There is no point in anything. That is the point.

The only truth you will ever need to understand is this body is not yours because you were never born into this world. You are not separate in any way from the universe. You are always and always have been a single reality, complete and just perfect as you are. Others who do not know this are like ghosts, mere fleeting shadows of what they are and could be. There is no division, no other, just original space. You, me, mine, yours, these are just conventions to live in the world. They have no real meaning.

You are not the sum of your senses which limit and confine you. But you have the potential to transcend the sensual word to be restored to your original space, which shines bright like an infinite sun. You are not your mind which is just a by-product of the imaginary process of living and dying. You and I, we don't have any separate physical identity. We don't even have a name. There is absolutely nothing to get hung up about.

There is no sense in trying frantically to understand any of this. You will just get caught up in the big ideas of your imagining. Let it all go and transform your sense of who you are into higher consciousness.

You are not your desires, opinions, and possessions. Do not get attached to them or let them take a hold on your free spirit. Your true nature has no qualities or attributes other than your perfection. You do not need any of the stuff that you have accumulated in your passage through life. Just know that you are already free and that the essence of your original face is freedom. Do not wear a mask and hide.

Everything in the world is illusory in that nothing compares to formless space. Your thoughts are just processes. In this imaginary world, things are constantly coming into existence and then going out of existence, like the mysteries of birth and death, which are products of the imagination.

Mystics down the ages have always spoken of the transcendental reality as ever the same, never changing. To understand this truth, all attachments in the mind have to be relinquished. Focusing on material objects only alienates us from our original space. In a state of pure consciousness, there can be no sense of existence or experience of anything other than consciousness. Oneness does not relate to anything because to relate is to divide.

When you live in a state of Oneness, there is no sense of existing or not existing. There is just consciousness. Mystics of the past have declared: *you are that. Not this, never this.* Other than consciousness, it is all an illusion. Everything is consciousness, even the dream of the world and all its charisma. Who am I to even speak of this? How can I talk about this reality as if it were something other than me?

I inhabit the original space of consciousness, formless. No relationship can condition this ultimate reality.

My true self is your true self which is this one shared reality. We delude ourselves that we have ownership of our personal reality. Suppose my sense of reality depends on me being there to experience it. What is it that remains when I am no longer there to share it?

Think of it as the space inside the glass. What happens to that space when the glass is shattered? It remains space. The glass is the illusion, and the space inside the glass is the mind, our sense of identity.

If your mind is bound to an illusory reality, it can be said not to exist because it is defined by something that is not real. So, who is doing the thinking? When your thoughts are known to be pure consciousness in action, you are free of any conceptualisation of what those thoughts are about. There is just thinking. Nothing exists that is not pure consciousness: no family, no society, no ideologies, no dogma, no politics. It is all pure consciousness, all a superior reality. Even the desire to be free is an attachment to a mind riddled with illusion. Who is there to be free? What is there to be liberated?

People get bogged down in fanciful ideas of what enlightenment means. They are happily devoted to their spiritual and religious belief systems, like a dog chasing its tail or an ox tied to a long rope. Our conditioning conditions all thoughts. The world we live in conditions every action. Reality is something else but is not anything that we can define. You can't say what truth is, just as you can't know what it is not. It is not black or white or any colour at all, not even waves of light or energy. I have not been involved in the world of senses and things. I am not even engaged in mortality. I am under no illusion about life. The glass is neither full nor empty but just imagination. Everything you do is imagination. Only the consciousness of creation is eternal and absolute. And because the world is all imagination, it is also eternally conscious.

This may seem a neat argument, but as such, it is meaningless unless it is referred to as insuperable consciousness that cannot be broken up into packets of information. Your logic proves nothing that was not already established. I value illogic as much as I love reason with dispassion and equanimity.

Knowledge knows itself. It is never wrong and never right but always just so. Neither male nor female, I am free of what must be learned. Your social manners mean nothing to me.

I am free of my body and claim no thoughts. I am the pure consciousness that is eternally real in a way that you cannot understand. You have to interact with the world because that is the way you have trained to do. Not I. I have cast that mantle and act in harmony with the one absolute reality not subject to the changing world. I am uninvolved with the relative world. So I do not experience anything other than consciousness.

I am not involved with the world of moving objects. I still know this is consciousness happening, but nothing happens. I am not a teacher or teach a method. I do not have a teacher or follow a technique. I exist and always will live, whether I am here or elsewhere. I am like the space in the glass. You and I, we have always been the same, timeless.

Consciousness is conscious of your original space, the unborn state. Still, you can never know this unborn state with your powers of intellect because you rely on your senses. Consciousness is present and unchanging in all dimensions and leaves no trace or ripples. It is the human condition to interact. We rely on names and characteristics to live in the world and construct our social reality as a collage. Imagine a world where there is just Oneness.

I am a mystic. I do not belong to this world, and I do not belong in any of the dimensions of human reality. I am the one single reality without beginning or end. When I die, nothing changes because I was never born. But I am alive with consciousness and have no desire or property or fancy clothes or any of the trappings of the human state. I do not live in your state of mind.

Am I confusing you? How can you understand the meaning of what I am saying except through your powers of reason? But I am telling you that you cannot reason your way to enlightenment. So how then to become enlightened?

Well, you don't need a teacher for this knowledge, and it's not in the books. I certainly can't tell you and have not the slightest inclination to do so. Mindfulness is a start but mindful of what? Reality is not conscious of anything other than consciousness. Inside, outside, physical, mental are all mental constructs. Consciousness is in everything and ever the same - even in the appearances of being different. To grasp that knowledge requires entering a transcended state of awareness. You see the universe shining both in reality and illusion and know there is no difference. In fact, there is no reality and no dream and diversity in appearance in this state of heightened consciousness. You can't take anything for real. Everything is an idealised version of whatever takes place in your brain.

As long as you think of yourself as a person with a mother, father, family, relations, friends, a place in society and carry emotional baggage, you will never understand what I am saying. If you think you have an immortal soul, you are digging an even deeper hole for yourself. Consciousness has no soul. Reality has no soul. Your original space is void of any concept, such as a soul or even the existence of a soul. What more is there to say? Nothing in this time-space continuum is of any importance, though it may seem so. Politics, referendums, elections? Forget them. They are all ideologies.

Even the word transcendental is misleading. How can oneness transcend itself? It is *sunyata,* zero, a void, shining and bright with consciousness, where nothing and everything happens simultaneously in a time vacuum.

My actions have no past and no future. Whatever I do is in the eternal present. This body is of no importance either because consciousness has no substance, neither light nor heavy. The sense of who I am is the biggest illusion of all. I am certainly not that person. I feel no shame or guilt. I don't even relate to the pain that this body experiences.

These are all words, and words cannot convey the immensity of the endless space, though you understand the concepts represented by terms. It is beyond the human brain to experience infinite space. The more I use words, the more you become caught up in big ideas.

I, too, have a body that will stop working one day, but that is not death. Need I say that death is an idea, and I have no sense of imagination. When my dear old body fails, I am going nowhere. I can't say that I am staying here either because I am not even here in the first place. Mystics of old call this state of being pure bliss consciousness. But don't take my word for it. As soon as you start to believe that what I am saying is true, you create a concept of truth. You think the truth is defined by being not false. Such thinking is division, more imagination that helps you make sense of the world.

Everything that you value I consider worthless: money, cars, fame, all pointless. I don't do anything except what is strictly necessary, and even then, I am not bothered in the slightest about the outcome. I wander through this world, free as a bird in the infinite sky. I don't follow the rules and regulations, and I don't break them either. You can keep your beloved intellect and logic. I am always peaceful, settled, happy and content. I want nothing because I have it all. You can also keep your transcendental meditation and your Yoga classes. I have already transcended what cannot be exceeded, and I have yogic unity with what cannot be divided. You see, I am the Avadhuta, the free mystic, and I am not human. I am just unconditioned consciousness in perpetual motion.

2 Reality

If you seriously want to understand the true nature of your reality by way of a teacher, do not dismiss anyone out of hand just because they don't look the part. A person may seem to you stupid or uneducated but still have something to offer. Don't make judgements based on appearance. The most unlikely sources of knowledge may present themselves to you if you keep an open mind. Some learned people lack the essence of knowledge – they know too much for their own good -. In contrast, an unsophisticated and straightforward person may be a channel for the immense power of consciousness.

There exists a higher intelligence that is still yet forceful, peaceful yet dynamic. This is the power of the universe. You are permeated with this higher intelligence which cannot be in essence anything other than pure consciousness, no matter what you do or think. It's not even a matter of choice. Pure consciousness does not have the infinitesimally slight trace of material existence and cannot be created, destroyed, or even conceived by you. Your brain is constantly active with molecular activity in the neuronal synaptic network, but thoughts arise and fall back into the vacuum of space, powered by consciousness. Your ego is like a bubble in a pond.

All differences derive from conditioned senses, which influence your brain, which causes feeling and sensation. At which point you believe that you are experiencing these sensations. You are experiencing consciousness, but you attribute this to something external as the source.

Mystics say that enlightenment is a gradual process and not a sudden flash of insight. It takes perseverance and practice to merge your innate intelligence with higher intelligence. You cannot use consciousness as an object of contemplation because there is nothing to hold onto. One tried and tested technique is to contemplate the subtler aspects of the physical world, such as the wind or sunlight or the flame of a candle.

Or focus on the processes of the senses in action: thinking, and not the thoughts, seeing and not the things see, hearing and not the things heard and so on. It becomes clear that everything is related. You gradually stop analysing and trying to pinpoint when something starts and finishes. When does something heard become a sound and when does it become hearing? When does the hearing create a mental image of what has been heard?

From waves of light, oscillations in the air, to impulses that travel down neuronal pathways, these subtlest processes happen a thousand times a` second, some at a level of the senses, others at a molecular level. Insight into these processes gradually becomes more incisive. Your individual consciousness frees itself from this brain activity and merges with unbound consciousness.

Your addiction to your idealised version of reality holds you down. For as long you are hooked on the trappings of the world, you will die with them. But suppose you free yourself of your addiction. In that case, you free yourself from the things that come in and out of existence, including your sense of identity and reality.

Your vision of reality is defined by the things around you, mental, visual, imaginary, remembered and physical. It is all experienced as the world, idealised or otherwise. There are so many philosophical definitions of what constitutes human reality, but these are of no importance. Everything experienced is finite human consciousness, even the concept of eternity.

Reality is the experience of that which has no appearance. You look up and see the moon and say correctly there is just one moon. You are compelled to define the moon by its position on the sky. So you create an appearance and compartmentalise the world. How else could you live? You must accept that your reality of multiplicities is illusory.

Consciousness is beyond human experience, but it nevertheless can be experienced. So you just got to stop thinking like a human. But you ask, how can I be anything other than human?

The point to grasp with your mind is that your natural state is pure consciousness and not the other way. This is where the illusion comes in. You believe it is natural to own things, be somebody and claim your place in the world. The economics of society depends on your needing stuff. This is not for your benefit and is a thoroughly unnatural situation. Give everything you own away, or at the very least stop buying. Your attachments to your possessions are pulling you deeper into a well of desire.

You end up working to support your lifestyle, a slave of your house and possessions. In working, you are constantly creating waves of human consciousness that keep the brain working overtime. You become stressed and lose sight of any reality other than your imaginations. To relax, you watch TV and get distracted. You live a life, and then you die. It is inevitable, and it is not so bad for most people. But it is a life in the shadows, a song played on a muted instrument. You die in fear or stupefied. What a waste.

Live a life devoted to your original space without any grandiose ideas of achieving anything. You will find peace of mind. You will live lightly like waves of energy until you dissolve into eternity and joy and bliss and absolute freedom.

When you live the life of the Avadhuta, you are not touched by desire, and you do not do anything motivated by selfishness. Your actions are pure and selfless, and you have no concerns. You do not get worked up about life. Your heart remains in the blissful cosmos. All relative knowledge, science, law, politics, economics, sociology, psychology, and other studies have nothing to teach you. Your only teacher is consciousness which reveals to you the birth of the universe and its passing into another dimension over billions of years and then dissolving into timeless space. Your attention is on the wave that rises and falls back into formless space.

You realise your true nature as the parade of life passes by you. This is because you are conditioned by a higher consciousness which is its own genesis. And so the ego comes to pass, with nothing to disrupt or disturb your serenity.

When the ego dissolves, so does your former self and you become realised, which means at one with tan unchanging reality. It is not complicated. There is nothing more to be learned, nothing to be aspired to. There is nothing to lose or gain. All differences cease to exist, even descriptions and words that were once useful: space, knowledge, pure, aware, conscious, higher, transcendental. There is nothing to be said or thought. This is the highest state that a person can achieve.

Nothing exists except this

I live a life of pure consciousness and know everything as waves of conscious energy, not like you who experience the world as a multiplicity of events happening simultaneously. I don't even experience the world as you do in comparative terms. This is so extreme that you will not understand this until you have gone beyond the human dimension. I must take a sledgehammer to shatter the bubble in which you live.

You must close your eyes and meditate, and eventually, you will understand just how transient this bubble world is.

There is no colour in my world. No gods and no worshipping. No devotion. No doubts and no questions or anxieties. There is just awareness of reality which presents itself as the world we all know, breathe and feel. I see the same world as you, but I know that this data stream is just a single unbroken flow. I know that I do not exist as anything other than data and molecules and energy. That is all there is. You may think you experience a different world, but this is not so. There is just consciousness, impersonal, featureless and empty. This is not some kind of quantum physics flow. This is a void where there is just consciousness which you and I use to create our cosmos.

If everybody in the world could get this, the world would act as a single mind. And it is not particularly hard to get this, but it goes against the grain of how you have learned to know the world around you, as well as your own mental universe.

You believe unquestioningly that there is a world of things to perceive. You know this world is made of opposites such as hold and cold, you and not you, day and night. Everything occupies its own space, and it is related somehow to everything else. What you don't see is that everything exists simultaneously.

What is happening is consciousness in action. Nothing else. You may dismiss me as a deluded fool. Or you call me a wise sage. I know that your reality is all relative. I don't deny your reality exists. I don't accept it exists either.

Can you accept that I ceased to be human when I abandoned my ego and ownership of my life? I surrendered to an existence neither day nor night, moving or still, good or bad, moral or immoral. I don't actually do anything. It is consciousness that does what you think I do. You may think I am a fantasist or a charlatan. But I can never describe what it is like to be me, without substance, beyond conditioned existence, immune to sorrow and grief, way beyond the reach of reason.

I am the calm waters in a pond, and I am the ripples caused by a passing dragonfly. I am that dragonfly and the sunlight falling on a nearby flower and the beating of the dragonfly's wings. You see beauty; I glimpse eternity. You see movement; I see consciousness in flux.

There is no point in any of this. None. I move through the world with no purpose, no ulterior motive. What for when everything is right here and now? Everything and nothing. Nothing exists except this.

Unknowing the world

You ask: how then do I experience the world if nothing exists? How to access this experience? One thing for sure is that worshipping statues, fetishizing icons, reciting mantras and burning incense will not shed any light on how consciousness operates. You can devote time and energy to contemplating on awareness. You can meditate or study. You can try Yoga exercises.

Left to your own imagination, you will live, and die ruled by your conditioned mind. Even the choices and decisions that you make are just reactions to unconscious conditioning. You fall back on your preferences which cause you to try to maximise pleasure and avoid pain. Perversely this generates degrees of the suffering of a psychological nature. Your mind is coloured by your preferences that create your psychosomatic self. You have an identity that you take to be yourself.

I have a mind too, but my mind has no colour and no preferences. I have an identity: that of pure consciousness which has no psychological nature. Consequently, I have no affiliation with knowledge or habits or choices or anything that could be construed as a personality. My mind is clear, like water or glass. Unfettered by the stuff that constantly presents itself and demands action to be taken, my mind is never anything other than pure consciousness. I call it an empty mind, not because it is void of thinking but because I have no sense of distinction. I call this Oneness.

Everything is the same, always the bright light of my original space. Breathing, thinking, remembering, thoughts, memories.

This original space did not evolve, nor did it manifest because I have never changed in a hundred billion years in this universe or the one before. I say our original space because we seem to share the same space but with different identities. There is no distinction: you and I are that authentic space.

We abide in universal consciousness, transcending what was never there. The paradox is complete. We live in a timeless space where nothing needs to be explained.

This is my conscious mind, now endlessly open, unattached to the dimensions of height and depth and perspective in time.

I see opportunities and possibilities.

I see opportunity born of imagination and all the consequences of my imagining.

I see new worlds where our physical world expands into all the combinations of energy that create an apparent reality where physical form dissolves into waves of thought; where thinking becomes an action-less action that assumes the appearance of a vast space that no words can ever describe.

Here nothing comes into being or goes out of being because there is just conscious existence. I walk through this world with no fixed ideas of who I am and what I believe. I am free of ideologies of hate and love. I see no walls, and I have no fear. Whatever comes is welcome to me. The past is never the past, and there is no future. There is only the conscious now.

People will tell you this and that. They will show you what is true and what is false. They will promote you or dismiss you as a naive dreamer. One person's reality is another person's dream. But I know that all of this is not happening outside of the human imagination. All your global wealth is just a dream creation and can disappear faster than a meteorite hitting the planet. I have transcended choosing between this and that, between true or false, boom or bust. I do nothing, not even choose. The world still goes on, and I sit here watching the river flow in pure consciousness.

My mind is the river, consciousness itself. Your conditioned mind is riddled with entrapments and experiments, caught in a race where there are winners and losers. If you do not acknowledge the race, there is no competition, and nobody wins or loses. Everybody is a winner.

I do not say anything because speaking is to enter your world of division, unity, love and hate, all ideologies. Space does not make a distinction between day and night, sun and moon. Consciousness does not get involved with desire or renunciation of desire. Even the very notions of doing anything or doing something are human conceptualisations. There is no judgement. You seek fame and fortune, but neither of these is what they claim to be.

Once you remove all distinction between this and that, you have mastered the art of knowing nothing. You see both the rain and the cloud, the tree and the book, and the imaginary world.

People struggle to let go of their self-identification with what they know and do. They have their team to support, their chosen profession, their skill sets and hobbies. Take this away, and their world is empty. But I am not saying that you must leave this behind. Everything you do is permeated with consciousness - it cannot be any other way. So carry on as before but know that you are do not doing anything.

The enjoyment and the disappointments will come and go but when you have taken the radical first step to identify yourself with higher consciousness, you do not suffer pain or loss.

Human consciousness operates on a limited scale of frequencies. Our optic nerves define our visual world. Consciousness is present in the entire spectrum of the material universe but cannot be measured in terms of frequency. I know this but am equally content in not knowing this. I don't claim to understand. How can you measure what has no beginning or end? It cannot be made or destroyed, or even identified. But its presence can be felt in the three fields of light, energy and mass.

A meditator is filled with light. A person who doubts will be plagued by doubt. A person who believes that the material world is the sum of all possible experiences will be weighed down by the past.

Your original space is not the body, although you think you are either dead or alive. Many abstract concepts or material things define the world. Why not drop this human conditioning which has you continually evaluating differences and dividing your world into multiple elements? Consciousness does not even have a name because it is neither a thing nor a concept.

I am just using words as that is what humans do. To be free, you have to drop all your ideas of the world and consciousness. Do nothing and let the universe do what it does best: expand and retract, endlessly conditioned to react. Consciousness does not respond. Neither do I react. I am the Avadhuta, pure consciousness, absolute and eternally free.

The One Mind

I wander the world dressed in whatever comes my way - rags, designer clothes, hand-me-downs. I do not aspire to live a life of virtue but follow an endless road free from prejudice and personal preferences. I do not distinguish between right or wrong, nor set myself any targets or goals to achieve. Instead, I realise the one truth that is not tainted by laws or moral codes. I see no point in discussing this. For me, it is self-evident.

I do not get bogged down in hopes and dreams. I do not sign up for organisations or groups or follow movements. Why, when consciousness is all that there is? Even talking about terms such as non-attachment or enlightenment is pointless. It is like trying to pin down a butterfly moving free against the backdrop of the sky. I say I follow the One Truth, but even that is misleading you into thinking something else exists other than this.

The world is constantly demanding that you make judgements and choices. I do whatever conditions dictate and do not care about the outcome because nothing happens in my state of consciousness, and I am not bound by causality. I live in awareness, with no ties to the physical and mental realms of the senses.

Some people spend their lives in spiritual contemplation, practising meditation and Yoga. Others dedicate their days to making the world a better place by creating a fairer society, eliminating disease, bigotry and oppression. This virtuous life is good, but until you, the collective human mind, realise that the world is already, in essence, a better place, these divisions will remain. Love and hate, greed and generosity, open borders and closed borders, us and them, all division.

The root cause of all injustice is the human mind, both the individual and the collective. Altruism is a sentiment imbued with the purity of truth, but it is still steeped in the sense of others. I have sacrificed my identity to eliminate that sense of their being anyone other than me as pure consciousness.

I have destroyed in my mind the concept that there exists anything other than consciousness. So I love the world but not as you do. I love the world for what it is not, not for what it is. Still, paradoxically, I love everything and everyone in the world because it is my original space, the source of human consciousness.

The truth of my existence is self-validating. To save the world, you have to destroy all ideas of there being anything other than consciousness. I love and respect you. I honour and praise you. I will care for you and protect you. Not for what you think you are but for the eternal consciousness that is your essence of being. One day may you be free too from the illusion of birth and death and the deep-rooted fear that conditions your choices and lifestyle. I am writing this as the embodiment of eternal consciousness so that you too may renounce your sense of who you are and realise your true potential.

VERSES ON THE TRUE MIND
THE THIRD PATRIARCH OF ZEN
HSIN HSIN MING BY SENG-T'SAN

Living is not difficult
If you hold no preferences.
When you neither like nor dislike,
Everything becomes clear and transparent.
But if you make the smallest distinction
Then you and your potential become divided.

If you wish to know your potential
do not judge or hold opinions.
Because clinging onto what we like and do not like
Is a fault line that runs through the mind.

When the meaning of reality is not understood,
The mind's natural state of stillness is needlessly disturbed.
Your mind is perfect, like infinite space
Where everything exists in equilibrium and harmony.

It is when we choose to accept or reject,
We do not see the true nature of things.
So do not get caught up in appearances.
Or in the abstract realm of emotions.

Be serene in your vision of oneness and
Your limited mindset will automatically dissolve.
But when you try to stop activity with non-activity
 Your very efforts fill you with activity.
If you stay polarised in one extreme or the other
You will never know your potential.

Those who do not live in perfect balance
Are victims of their actions and thoughts,
And fall victim to assertion and denial.

To deny the reality of things
Is to miss their reality.
To assert the emptiness of things
Is to miss their reality.

The more you talk and think about anything,
The further you stray from the truth.
Just stop talking and thinking,
And there is nothing you will not be able to know.

Do not search for the truth.
Only cease to value opinions.
Do not remain in the dualistic state.
Do not chase the world.

If there is even a trace of duality,
Of right and wrong, of them and us,
Of now and then, lost and found,
You will be trapped in opposites.

Although all dualities come from the One,
Do not be attached even to this One.
When the mind exists uninvolved,
Nothing in the world can cause trouble.
And the world ceases to exist as before.

When no discriminating thoughts arise,
The old mind ceases to exist.

When thought objects dissolve,
The thinking ego dissolves:
As when the mind dissolves, things dissolve.

Things are objects because of the mind:
Things condition the mind.
When you understand the relativity of the mind and its
objects,
You know the underlying reality: the unity of Emptiness.

In this Emptiness, the world becomes one
And mind and matter contain the whole world.
Prejudice and opinion hold no attraction.

To live in Endless Space is neither easy nor difficult.
But those who are trapped in the world are heavy in mind:
The faster they hurry, the slower they go.

Even to be attached to the idea of enlightenment
Is to be caught in the web of the world.

Just let things be in the world as they are
And there will be neither coming nor going.
Know the nature of things and your nature,
And you will pass through life freely and undisturbed.

When the mind is in bondage, truth is hidden
And everything is covered by shadow and fog.
Just living in a world of opinions
Is unsatisfactory and troublesome.

What lasting benefit can be had
From this parade of transient glory?
If you wish to live in the space of the One
Do not even try to shun the world of senses and ideas.

To accept the world as space,
But knowing that space is not the world,
Is the mind of enlightenment.

The wise person does not try to achieve anything.
The foolish person is caught up in self-imposed knots.

Peace and disharmony stem from illusion.
With enlightenment, there is no liking and disliking.
All this division comes from opinionated ignorance,
Like catching dreams or grasping flowers in the air.

It is plain stupid to try to pin them down
 Like the wings of a butterfly.
Win or lose, success or failure,
You must abandon such concepts forever.

If the eye never sleeps,
The dreaming will naturally cease.
If your mind does not get lost in duality,
You will know the objective world for what it is:
Manifestations of a single essence.

To understand the mystery of this One Being
Is to be released from the web of the world.

When all things are experienced equally
The timeless Self is reached,
No comparisons or analogies are possible
In this causeless, relationless state.

Movement becomes still
And there is stillness in motion.

There is only stillness in movement.

To this ultimate truth, there is no dogma or proof.
For the mind rooted in a vision of Oneness
All self-centered striving ceases.

Doubts and fears dissolve,
And living in trust and faith becomes settled.
In a single moment, we are set free from bondage:
Nothing clings to us, and we adhere to nothing.
All is empty, clear, and self-effulgent.

The mind does not seek to impose itself on the world.
There is neither self nor other-than-self.

In the vision of oneness, thought, feeling, knowledge, and
imagination are known as mere fleeting phenomena.

To experience a vision of this reality
Just say when doubt arises, "not two".
In this "not two", nothing is separate, nothing is excluded.

Always there, enlightenment means entering this truth.
And this truth is beyond modification in time and space:
A single thought is ten thousand years.

Emptiness is everywhere, but the infinite universe
Exists before your eyes, infinitely large and infinitely minute,
Undifferentiated, all attributes have dissolved.

No beginning or end is known.
So too with existence and non-existence.

Don't waste time in doubts and questions.
One thing, everything, moves in the same space.

To live in this realisation is to live without any fear of
imperfection.
To live in this trust and faith is to travel the path to non-
duality,
Because the non-dual is one with a trusting mind.

But these are just words!
The Vision of Oneness is beyond language.

There is no past
No future, no dreaming
All is consciousness.
This is your potential greatness.

Exercises in awareness

Exercise 1

Awareness of Sound

This exercise should be done with the eyes closed, though eyes open also works.

Five minutes

Be aware of sound. Simply be mindful that sound exists, independent of what we are hearing. Whatever is being listened to is sound. Take time off from associating sound with things and objects and creating more associations with other things and objects. Instead, be aware of Pure Sound.

Exercise 2

Five minutes Awareness of Logic

This exercise can be done with the eyes open or closed. It makes no difference. It is an exercise in awareness.

Be aware of the force of logic in your life. Do not evaluate the rights and wrongs or the consequences. Simply be mindful that logic exists.

Exercise 3

Ten minutes Awareness of Higher Consciousness

This exercise can be equally done with eyes closed or open. With eyes closed is closer to the meditative experience and is more focused on mental awareness. If doing with eyes open, it is best to fix on a single point. The awareness is more visual.

The point of this exercise is to start to 'know' higher Consciousness. Gradually an awareness rises that there is a greater power observing what's going on.

Exercise 4

Asmita – self-identity

This exercise is with eyes closed and open. The practice is slightly different.

With eyes closed, this is more meditative. Be aware of your sense of being someone- your I-am-ness. Before your self-identity. Your sense of existence is a person who knows the world. Find that I-am-ness and stay with it

Do not get distracted by your thoughts or your name. Just enjoy the experience of being alive without all the stuff that gets attached to you.

Exercise 5

The sixth sense and duality

Be aware of the mind in operation. Do not conclude or judge. Awareness is open-ended, a string of moments in a continuum.

With eyes closed, be aware of the associations that give meaning and value. How the mind gives rise to a sense of self from I-am-ness. The likes and dislikes, the preferences, and aversions. Do not go too deep into the mind – just be aware that you have a sense of mind, and that mind is not you.

With eyes open, see how a sixth sense is constantly processing the world. Observe the mind as a process, reacting, associating, conceptualising and objectifying,

Exercise 6

Awareness of thought

Close your eyes to filter out visual stimulation. Observe how thoughts associate with memory, sound and other thoughts, creating a sequence of ideas and images. Do you have control over this process?

The gist of this exercise is not to control your thoughts or the mind, but simply to be aware of what's going on. In time, a guiding principle becomes apparent – the power of association. And your ability to associate with ever more profound levels of experience opens up hitherto hidden fields of potential and opportunity.

Exercise 7

Awareness of Karma

Awareness of Consciousness is not measured by facts and figures, nor can it be understood in terms of ideas and concepts.
We can observe the flow of karma in the world, be they human or natural. Cars, voices, wind, leaves rustling, the play of light from the sun. We are aware as an impartial witness who is 'knowing' the world, not judging, but not associating or engaging.

Exercise 7-2

Awareness of Potential

Be aware of how everything is changing every second. This is the principle of change. Even in the elusive timeless Now there is change. And herein lies the power of potential. Be aware of change and trust that in change you will find opportunities.

There is no forcing the issue here. Simply be aware of the flux of existence. It takes practice to not interfere with the process but just let change unfold without our intervention. Eventually, we learn to impartially observe events as they unfold, even if for a limited time of thirty minutes, before diving back into the maelstrom of human activity.

Exercise 8

Awareness of Higher Self

Be aware of the multiplicity of objects and things experienced in the waking state are anchored in the divided and partial reality. On the other hand, the senses define how the world is known, giving rise to the illusion that the world experienced through the senses is an individual experience.

Exercise 9

Awareness of Vivek

30 minutes

Be aware of how the whole universe appears to be coming into existence and going into a state of dissolution, just as bubbles of water appear and disappear in the ocean. The forms of plants and trees appear from light and in the end, disappear into light.

Be aware of the essential and non-essential, purposeful and purposeless.

Exercise 10

Awareness of Opportunity

Meditating with awareness of higher consciousness establishes in you a sense of potential greatness wherever you go or whatever you do. You see your path clearly and the direction that you are travelling in. You feel no need to alter or change because just by being aware of the power of a higher consciousness in your life sets you right. Just like water finds its level, so too will you find your balance.

Do not dwell on thoughts or revelations or insights. And don't try to remember or claim. Simply be aware and the rest will follow.

Printed in Great Britain
by Amazon